PLANNING YOUR
Organic
VEGETABLE GARDEN

PLANNING YOUR Organic VEGETABLE GARDEN

DICK KITTO

Line illustrations by Nils Solberg

Colour photography by Sue Stickland and
the Henry Doubleday Research Association

Thorsons
An Imprint of HarperCollins*Publishers*

Thorsons
An Imprint of HarperCollins*Publishers*
77–85 Fulham Palace Road,
Hammersmith, London W6 8JB

Published by Thorsons 1986
5 7 9 10 8 6 4

© Dick Kitto 1986

Dick Kitto asserts the moral right to
be identified as the author of this work

A catalogue record for this book
is available from the British Library

ISBN 0 7225 1104 3

Printed in Great Britain by
Woolnough Bookbinding Limited,
Irthlingborough, Northamptonshire

CONTENTS

CHAPTER 1
WHY PLAN?

Few people take a lot of trouble over the planning of their kitchen garden and very few books give planning more than the most cursory treatment. This is a pity, because, although a hit and miss approach is good enough for someone who is content to use the odd corner to grow lettuces or strawberries in, it can be very wasteful for those who want to make the most of the space they have available. Eventually, however, people do realize that it is worth making quite an effort to increase the crops they are able to obtain from their plot and from the work they put in.

Planning can benefit you in various ways according to how seriously you take it and how much time and trouble you put into it. It can consist merely of sitting down one winter evening with a seed catalogue, pencil and paper, and making a rough list of what you are going to grow next season and how much seed you will need. Or, at the other end of the scale, it can involve working out a very exact plan of what you are growing this year, where you are growing it, when it will be sown, planted and harvested, and what will follow it in subsequent years.

Full-scale planning involves not only time and trouble, but also taking a rather disciplined approach to gardening; this can become second nature once you are used to it, but in the early days can lead to confusion, being perhaps more than most people are able

to tackle. At some stage, when you have a little experience of what is involved, it is wise to sit down and take stock, and decide just how ambitious you wish to be and how much time you are prepared to give to planning. Here perhaps it is worth suggesting that you do not plunge initially into complicated plans with too much enthusiasm. It might be better to ease yourself in gradually so that you get used to the general approach as you go along. Do not lose sight of the fact that although the challenge of using every bit of space to produce the maximum crop of good vegetables is very much a part of the pleasure of gardening, it is not worth becoming obsessional about it.

So what are the benefits of planning, how much extra work is required and how complicated is it? In this chapter I intend to give a very brief summary of the main benefits before considering each of them in detail later in the book.

The benefits of planning are:

1. *To grow crops in the best position* both from the point of view of the best aspect as well as the greatest convenience. This requires quite a bit of thinking ahead and forward planning. It is surprising how often people seem, almost per-versely, to grow some crops in a way that militates against success. To take an obvious example, you must have the foresight to anticipate that in May you may want to use a sunny spot for

tomatoes, so you should not sow peas there in March. Or that it may be better to grow crops that suffer pigeon damage close to the house so that you are on hand to take retaliatory action (even if retaliation against pigeons is a bit of a forlorn hope). Or that it may be quite pleasant in summer to have to walk the length of the garden for a sprig of parsley, but what about the winter months when it is cold, probably raining, and it gets dark before anyone arrives home to start cooking the evening meal?

2. *To ensure space is not wasted*, for example by growing more of one crop than you need to the eventual exclusion of another that you lack. You must make sure that there is always sufficient ground ready for sowing or planting when you want it. With the coming of spring and a sudden flush of warm days and gentle fresh breezes, people creep out of the dark caverns in which they have over-wintered and stretch up to the bright sunshine and the promise of summer to come. Enthusiastically they clear off the weeds, dig and level and rake and sow row upon row of summer vegetables. A few months later they are swamped with an abundance of lettuces going to seed and peas in profusion, followed closely by huge crops of runner beans, courgettes and tomatoes far beyond their capacity to consume or freeze, and which they cannot even give away because everyone else is similarly glutted. Meanwhile their garden is so overcrowded with herbage that there is no room to sow or plant autumn and winter vegetables, which are therefore crowded into some dark corner where they struggle skywards for light.

What you obviously need from the very start of the season is to have a clear idea of the crops you want to grow for autumn and winter, when they need to be planted or sown, and where you are going to grow them. Your early summer plantings must allow for this, and in some cases your ambitions for the winter must bend towards your summer needs or vice versa. This is one of the basic planning operations from which the others stem. It is not too complicated a process, but it does require thought and calculation in advance, a list of required crops and a reasonably accurate plan of your garden.

3. *To ensure a continuous succession of crops* over their season. This really derives from point 2, above.

4. *To ensure that whatever compost and manure you have available is used when and where it is most effective.* This extends planning into another dimension – not just what you grow and where and when you grow it, but also maintaining your soil in a state of maximum fertility.

Some home gardeners practise organic methods, using no chemical fertilizers or pesticides. A majority perhaps still resort to chemicals, either as a matter of course or when there seems to be a pressing need – though the mood is changing not only among home gardeners but among professional growers and even farmers. And most gardeners who use chemicals recognize the need for ample supplies of organic matter as well. The bias of this book is towards organic methods, not only because these are what I have always believed to be best, and have always practised, but because I think there is a growing reaction amongst gardeners against the use of chemicals.

But the problem is this: How do you maintain a sufficiently plentiful supply of organic fertilizer, manure and compost? On a rough count of allotments I have visited, about one in four allotment holders make their own compost – some of them, to be honest, in a rather haphazard fashion. Also, about two in three have a load of manure delivered every year – usually a three- or four-ton load of pig or poultry manure from an intensive unit which is all most people are able to get hold of. But even for these people the problem remains – there is never enough.

In the heyday of organic gardening the growers in the Lea Valley (and, of course, elsewhere) used up to 100 tons of horse manure per acre every year. For an average allotment measuring approximately 90 feet long by 30 feet wide (27 by 9m) this works out at six or seven tons of compost a year. That is to say, that is the amount you will need to maintain the soil in a state of fertility. If, as is quite likely, the ground is in a fairly run-down state when you first start to work it, you could well need twice that amount for several years to bring it up to scratch. This is, of course, not beyond the bounds of possibility, but in practice nearly everyone finds that there is never enough compost to go round. So, an important part of planning is to ensure that whatever supply of organic matter you can lay your hands on is used when and where it is most effective.

5. *To enable you to grow some green manure crops* on vacant land is, of course, a contribution to this need for organic matter. It is a very worthwhile contribution, but is definitely an 'extra' – something to be thought about when everything else is running smoothly. Many gardeners have come round to the understanding that the time-honoured advice to dig in the autumn and leave the ground roughly ridged for the frost to act on, although un-doubtedly of some benefit in creating a surface tilth for the next season, is

probably mistaken. Equally, the sight of a bare expanse of brown earth with a few young crops growing in splendid isolation rather like cactuses in the Arizona Desert offends the first principle of nature: it is the green carpet of the earth that has created and still maintains the fertility of the soil upon which we all depend. Growing a crop to maintain that fertility is not only right in principle but was for a long time standard agricultural practice, and it still makes sense.

6. *To save on the annual cost of seed,* and thus ensure that you can always afford a good spread of the varieties you need. This may seem a bit incidental to general planning but it is certainly very well worth doing. Again, it is not necessary, or wise, to become fanatical about it. It is mainly a matter of taking a little care to be orderly and well organized. Buying seeds can be expensive and costs can soon mount up if you are growing forty or fifty different varieties. Quite a lot of the seed may be wasted unnecessarily by not being stored with sufficient care to ensure reasonable germination.

There are three ways of saving money on seeds; the first is to join with other people and buy your seeds collectively as a group. Although an obvious economy, this requires some-one with not only a bit of organizing ability to get the system going, but also with the will to do so. In fact I know very few groups that manage to do it successfully. A variant of this is to buy through your local horticultural or allotment society – well worth doing, as it can give you a considerable discount on your packets of seed. This can supplement, but need not replace, the two other methods. The second way of being economical with your seeds is to keep every packet of seed for the whole of its useful life in such conditions that it retains high germination. The third is to allow certain crops to grow to seed-bearing stage and save the seed. I think that with only a minimal amount of care most people's seed bills could be reduced by as much as two-thirds. This not only saves money, but encourages people to lay out a little more in order to experiment with a wider selection of crops.

7. *To establish a rotation of crops over the years* so that plants of the same family or group are not grown in the same place in successive years. This is the 'rotation' to which passing reference is often made in gardening books. It derives originally from the four-year rotation which used to be practised in farming and perhaps still is by a dwindling number of small farmers. What works on a farming scale, however, does not necessarily or easily transfer to the scale of the allotment or back garden, and to carry it out effectively is not nearly so simple as it is made out to be. For whereas the other aspects of planning discussed in this book are really no more than a process of introducing some degree of order and foresight into your gardening, crop rotation does involve proper planning over the years. This, in turn, involves a structured approach and a fair amount of discipline in adhering to your plans. The pros and cons of planning a crop rotation are considered in Chapter 9. In the earlier chapters I have tried to keep things simple and to take account of people's varying degrees of commitment, time and energy, so that the first part of the book can be read without any need to contemplate, let alone understand or practise, the more complex problems of a proper rotation.

CHAPTER 2
THE SITE

Before you can tackle any detailed aspects of planning, you must first consider the site of your garden and decide how to make the best use of it. Most people do not have much choice over this: they have an allotment of standard size or they live in an urban or suburban area where every house has an identical long narrow rectangle of garden. They will probably have a patio and perhaps a lawn adjacent to the house and beyond it, or adjacent to it, a flower garden or rockery, and if there is any spare room near the house herbs will be given priority. The space for vegetables is likely to be a narrow strip down one side or a rectangle at the end. The amount of shade may be quite out of your control due to outside trees and buildings, access to the garden may be restricted, and the needs and demands of other members of the family (including the dog) may limit the size and site of the vegetable garden.

Obviously one of the first things to do is to establish priorities: the sunny spot in the garden cannot simultaneously accommodate a wistaria, a vine, a peach tree and a dozen tomato plants. Are flowers or fruit or vegetables to have first choice, or is it possible to combine two uses; for example, by training a peach tree along a sunny wall and growing tomatoes or peppers in front of it?

Then, there is the question of *slope*. Is the ground level? If it slopes, in which direction does it do so? Obviously a slope to the north is undesirable, especially if it is combined with shade: it could seriously delay your soil warming up in the spring and make your garden a late frosty one. If it has a steep slope to the north it would be a good idea to think of terracing it; even a small area terraced more or less level in which you concentrated your early crops or those that need warmth, might be worth it. It would be wise to site this adjacent to a path, as the soil for one or two feet north of it may be in the shade for most of the day (Figure 1).

If your garden slopes south this is a tremendous bonus which you must take full advantage of, so long as the slope is not so steep that it makes working difficult. Do not forget that as you cultivate sloping ground the topsoil will tend inevitably to move down the slope, and this tendency must be counteracted by always moving the soil back upwards when digging, hoeing, raking, etc.

With any sort of slope beware of one problem: everyone knows that hot air rises – and the corollary of this is that cold air sinks. If your garden slopes, cold air will sink or roll down it until it is held up by an obstacle. If there is no escape downwards it will stay put and settle like a pool of icy water, and if it is cold enough it will create a frost pocket (Figure 2). So – do not have any

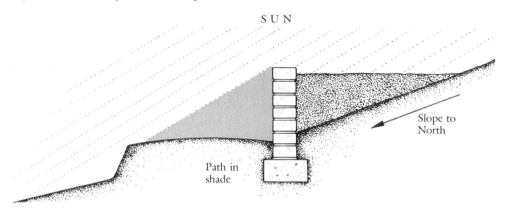

obstacles if you can help it, and if you cannot help it perhaps you had better use it to grow parsnips, celery or Jerusalem artichokes, all of which are improved by frost, or swedes, savoys or kale which are pretty impervious to it.

Of course, if you are terracing a north slope, as suggested above, be very careful that in terracing your beds southwards, you are not creating a frost pocket there. One way to ensure this is to raise the terracing in the centre so that the terraced ground, as well as sloping south, also slopes away from the centre towards the two edges. The cold air will then, in its journey downwards, float or roll to each side and slip round the edges. Figure 3 shows quite a steep slope from the centre to the edges in order to emphasize this. In fact, only the gentlest of slopes is needed to ensure that the cold air rolls down it.

It is worth considering whether there is enough *space* near the house to grow not just your major culinary herbs but some of the most frequently used salad vegetables as well. Also, what sort of flower garden are you going to have – should you aim to grow some vegetables in it? Globe artichokes, cardoons, runner beans, red orache and borage are some of the attractive large vegetables that would not look out of place. Parsnips, salsify, scorzonera, fennel, chicory, leeks and onions all have interesting flowers or seedheads if left to produce seed; and some lettuces,

Figure 2: How cold air sinks to form frost pockets

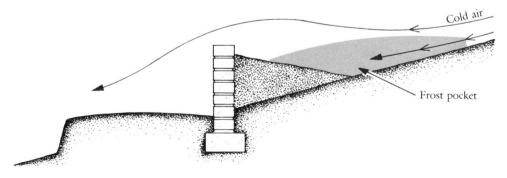

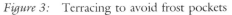

Figure 3: Terracing to avoid frost pockets

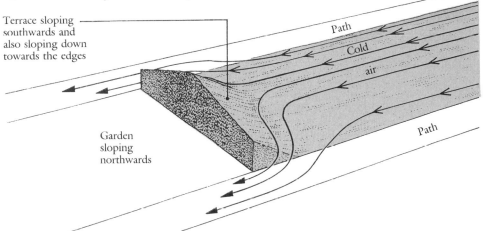

Terrace sloping
southwards and
also sloping down
towards the edges

Path

Cold

air

Path

Garden
sloping
northwards

chicories and other green salad plants have attractive foliage. Then, what about the more revolutionary idea of having flowers in the vegetable garden, with the vegetables selected partly for their decorative appearance as well as their eating quality? Of course, this is not all that revolutionary: it was common in French and English gardens in the seventeenth century and has faded out with different fashions in flower gardens. I do not see why it should not be revived – it is certainly possible to make a vegetable garden attractive and this may encourage you to feel that the vegetables do not have to be hidden away behind a hedge out of view of the house but can come out into the open and encroach upon some of the ground originally allocated to flowers.

Next, we must consider the question of *shelter*. The prevailing wind from the south west can do a lot of damage in the summer, blowing to the ground peas and runner beans which have been staked inadequately and playing havoc with sweet corn, broad beans, brussels sprouts and many other plants. But it is the bitter north-easters in the spring that probably do the most damage as

they descend upon tender, newly emerging crops. One difficulty is that the wind does not always blow in where you expect it to; in urban areas, especially, it is often funnelled by buildings, and swooshes turbulently from quite unexpected directions. So, before you start taking protective measures, spend some time in your garden on windy days identifying in which directions the wind will blow.

Then, try to think what is the best form of protection, but do not forget the warning in the previous section: whatever shield you erect against the wind can also, if carelessly placed, be a shield against the escape of freezing air. It may be necessary to leave a gap for the cold air to slip through (Figure 4). If the wind is very bad you may have to create a double barrier.

Now let us look at the various forms of protection.

A wall or solid fence. This may do the trick but, on the other hand, it may block the wind altogether, causing the wind to spiral upwards and downwards and create an area of turbulence on your side as well as on the other. It might be a good idea to get some temporary

Figure 4: Erecting a double wind barrier to avoid creating a frost pocket

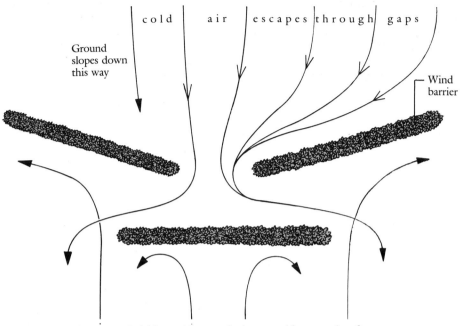

cold   air   escapes through gaps

Ground
slopes down
this way

Wind
barrier

Prevailing wind blows this way: hedges provide protection from
wind but enable cold air to escape downwards

fencing or even a sheet or so of old hardboard and try them in position to see their effect before you put up anything permanent.

A hedge. Perhaps a hedge is the best solution, but the touble is, of course, that it will take up space and, even if clipped back, its roots will extend outwards, creating an area where not much will grow. Also a hedge will constitute just one more candidate for your care and attention, and initially can be quite a drain on your pocket.

Fine plastic netting. This provides a surprisingly effective windbreak, calming down turbulent winds but still allowing a flow of fresh air into the garden. It is the most effective protection against vagrant cats too – in urban areas they are probably more of a menace to gardens than the occasional gale.

A trellis. This has similar advantages though it will not keep out cats, and will not last as long as plastic. But you can use it to train climbers on, making it more useful and decorative than some other solutions.

Lastly you can leave the gap and so plan your garden that at the crucial times there are always vegetables growing there to provide a screen. Suitable vegetables are Jerusalem artichokes (summer to late autumn); spinach and seakale beet left to go to seed but still pickable (May–June); or sunflowers (midsummer to autumn) – not a vegetable (unless you save the seed) but good compost material. Of course, crops like maize, runner beans, and maincrop peas also provide a very good windbreak but, as they themselves are subject to wind damage, planting them in such a position would be like robbing

Peter to pay Paul. But the following is quite a good combination. In the gap, as close to the boundary as possible, grow spinach beet (which you pick from your side). In the spring when it goes to seed keep it cut down to between 4 and 5 feet. About 18 inches (45cm) inwards sow or plant your runner beans, providing them with a sturdy structure to support them. As soon as the beans are well established (which should be by late June), lift the beet (preferably by chopping them off at ground level with a sharp spade, so as not to disturb the soil around the beans) in order to provide access for picking the beans. In this space you can, if you like, grow a quick maturing crop of green manure which will keep the weeds down and provide a carpet to walk on.

If you have an allotment, which is almost certain to be fairly open exposed land, it is best to have a look and see what other people have done. The odds are that most people will have done nothing, but search around, for even among allotment-holders there are only a few dedicated gardeners – and, anyway, when you first get an allotment it pays to wander around to see which crops are being grown and how well they do.

The *soil* is not always what it looks. For example, up to the First World War and even in many places up to the Second World War, many large towns (including London) were surrounded by market gardens which supplied them with their vegetables. In later years, and especially with the post-war housing boom, the value of land rocketed and it became more profitable to sell the land for development. So, many houses in the suburbs are built on first class market-garden land that was cultivated for hundreds of years. Others are built on the sites of bomb damage or demolished factories, etc., in which case a thin veneer of what looks superficially like first-class soil may camouflage a base of assorted builders' rubble. Still others – perhaps new developments close to the green belts – may still contain the original soil which was under grass and not cultivated for years. It is important to know which you have; indeed, your garden may contain patches of different kinds.

First of all examine the surface – do plants and weeds grow well? Is the soil sour-looking – bluish or greyish – or is it a healthy dark brown? Does it have moss? Does it look waterlogged? Dig a hole in it at least 18 inches (45cm) deep. How hard was the digging operation? If it was very hard it may be due to the quality of the soil, or it may be that you have chosen to dig in a spot that has been heavily trodden down. Try another spot just to make sure. Slice down the edge of your hole so that it presents a smooth clear profile. Can you see roots there or other debris? Worm holes? Or other evidence of organic matter? Take some damp soil from the top 3 inches in your hand and rub it between your palms and fingers into a ball. Is it firm and soft, neither very sticky nor gritty, holding together but quite easy to break into crumbs, but then easy to re-form into a ball? If so, you are lucky, it is a good garden loam with a reasonably high organic content.

Or does the soil feel very coarse and gritty, and does it fall apart easily? In that case it is a sandy soil, easy to work, quick to warm up in the spring, but liable to dry out in the summer just at the time when you are forbidden to use sprinklers. And it will require very large and frequent additions of organic matter to maintain its fertility. It will also probably require frequent liming.

Or does it hold together a bit like wet

putty or glue? Be careful now, because two very different types of soil form wet sticky balls and the distinction between them is important. One is clay, and a clay soil is stiff and sticky with a surface which when wet is like a coating of glue. When it is dry and you break it up it will remain in quite hard lumps. The other is silt: when it is wet it feels slippery and silky but not gluey; when it is dry it is hard, often very hard, but once you have broken it up it will crumble apart and can easily be reduced to dust. The difference between the two is as follows:

Clay is formed by the pulverisation of rock, and most clays (though not all) consist of flat particles rather like sheet glass. The particles stick together just as two sheets of glass stick together when they are damp. The addition of sand, provided it is well mixed and integrated into the soil will help clay to flocculate and form a fine tilth on the surface because the sand will help to separate the interface of the clay (Figure 5).

Another characteristic of clay soils is that the molecules have an electric charge. Without going into technical details this means that the addition of

such salts as lime (which also have an electric charge) helps clay to flocculate and create a surface which can be worked into a good tilth for seeding. Liming is, in fact, a standard practice to increase the working quality of clay soils. Be careful, though, to check the acidity of the soil first, because a few clays (including some of the Thames Valley clays) are already alkaline, and the addition of the lime will make them more so. They may become too alkaline for most vegetables to grow satisfactorily. For these alkaline clays, instead of adding lime you should add gypsum, which has the same benefits without increasing the soil's alkalinity.

Silt particles tend to be round like sand, but are very much smaller (though they are not nearly so small as clay). They form hard lumps with the sand by a process of packing and wedging between the sand particles (Figure 6). It is for this reason that the addition of sand will not improve silty soils; organic matter is the best improver for them. Many of the soils commonly regarded as clays are, in fact, silts. Silt is much more often met with

Figure 5: Clay and sand

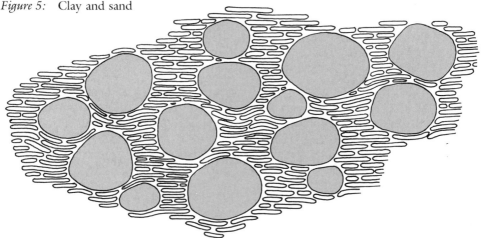

Figure 6: Silt and sand wedged solidly together

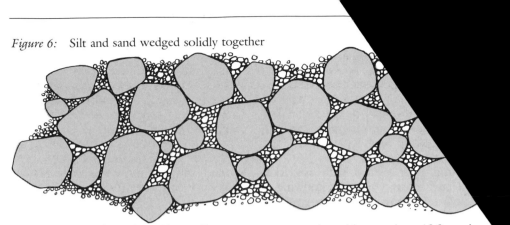

in British soils than clay. Clay soils are actually comparatively rare in this country.

The composition and characteristics of different soils is a very complex subject, and the summaries above are superficial and generalized. They are no more than a rough and ready guide, which can, however, be useful for the gardener.

The top spit can be deceptive when judging the quality of soils. For example, it is quite common, especially in gardens that have been cultivated for some time, for the top spit to be a reasonably fertile silty loam or silty clay loam, while beneath this is a hard rock-like layer which is inpenetrable to roots and will not drain. Fill the hole you have dug with water and see how quickly it drains. Stick your fork into the bottom of the hole and, by gently working it back and forth as you press down with your foot, try to insert it further. If it will not go easily, and if the water is slow to drain, you may be in for trouble. Try to dig down a bit deeper – say 2 or 2½ feet – to see. If there is a hard pan you may have to double dig the whole plot and incorporate a lot of bulky compost or manure. If you do not have enough manure or compost, or do not fancy double digging, you had better explore the garden further and see if conditions are better elsewhere. On the other hand, if the hard pan seems to be widespread, or if for other reasons there is no alternative, I suggest you take the remedial action described in Chapter 6.

Then, try knocking a 1 inch (2.5cm) diameter pipe into the ground (or use a crowbar if you have one) in various spots to see how far and how easily it penetrates. It is worth knocking it in for quite a short distance (say, 6 inches, 15cm) right across the width of the garden to see if there are any hard gravel or concrete paths hidden beneath the surface. If you do find one you had better trace its journey and decide whether to leave it or go to the trouble of digging it up.

All this exploration is to help you to decide which part of your garden to allocate to vegetables and where to put your garden shed, compost heap, lawn, etc. It will, of course, also help you to decide on any treatment needed for the area you do choose. Naturally what you are aiming for is a sheltered open sunny spot with a good depth of brown, fertile, crumbly, loamy soil.

The vegetables do not all have to be grown in one area – that may be convenient but does not necessarily make the best use of what is available. If there are one or two separate beds you may care to use these for permanent crops (rhubarb, asparagus, Jerusalem artichokes – not really a permanent

were) so as
one area.
a special
though
s most
wing
veen

ɔu have
much you can
each crop. So, once
size and shape you can
to make some calculations. But
there is one factor that will affect this
and needs to be thought about early on,
and that is which growing system you
are going to use. This really boils down
to a choice between the bed system and
the row system.

In the *row system* your whole garden is
divided by a small number of paths —
perhaps just one down the centre. The
plots between the paths are quite large
and are marked off in rows. Access to
the rows for cultivation, planting, harvesting, etc., is gained by walking over
the beds, taking care to tread between
the rows of growing crops. At a guess,
90 per cent of all the gardens in Britain
are cultivated on this system.

In the *bed system* the garden is divided
by numerous paths into small beds
whose narrow width allows you to
reach the whole bed from the path. The
bed system is, of course, quite an old
one but its recent popularity has come
about in the wake of several systems of
raised bed gardening which were developed partly to make lighter work of
bending down to attend to plants, and
partly to enable the gardener to reach
easily to the centre of the beds without
having to tread on the actual bed, which
it was felt compacted the soil too much
and destroyed its structure. But in

practice most people have found that
raised beds do not really work very well.
For one thing they have a natural
tendency to become flat beds, the
original nice semi-circular mound slow-
ly sinking and shedding its edges down
on to the paths. Since the paths are the
lowest part of the plots they usually
double up as drainage channels when
there is heavy rain, so the soil is carried
away to the ditches, or wherever the
paths drain to. Thus, to maintain these
beds you need to be continually throw-
ing the earth back from the path, or else
you need to contain them with wood or
some other material. But, as the beds
are small and narrow, they (and thus
their edges) will also be numerous, so
containing them will involve great
quantities of wood and work. Another
problem with raised beds is that in areas
of low rainfall (for example, East
Anglia) they tend to dry out — well,
more than tend to, they *do* dry out even
in a quite ordinary summer. Luckily
East Anglia does not seem to suffer
from water shortages to the same extent
as the rest of the country, but watering
with a sprinkler or watering can tends
to wash away the edges of the raised
beds even more than the rain does.

The further reasoning in favour of
raised beds is our increased understanding that for maximum crops plants
should be grown much closer together
than was formerly believed. Rows 12 or
18 inches (30–45cm) apart were designed more for the convenience of
mechanical cultivation and of access
between the rows than for the needs of
the plants. Also, a variety of crops in
one area, with different heights and
spread of leaves, may have advantages
over single crops. When you do grow a
single crop it is more economical to
grow it broadcast in a hexagonal pattern
than in rows. Much of this thinking
seems to make good sense and, as a

result, the bed system has remained, replacing to some extent the raised bed system – though even now bed systems are only rarely found. I do not think I have ever seen an allotment grown on the bed system – but then we allotment-holders do tend to be an aged and conservative group of people.

Then there is the question: How important is it never to step on the soil? F.L. King, the pioneer of the no-digging system, used to say that a small army of visitors would visit his garden every month and walk all over the beds without doing any harm to the soil, which was so fertile that it had the resilience of a sponge. Well, maybe – after all he had worked in the same garden for forty years or so and did not have any problems about supplies of organic matter.

A lot of gardens I have seen have had the resilience of concrete and some of this may well have been due to, or been aggravated by, being walked over. It is so hard to be sure of this. Agreed that a poor quality clay or silt soil will become very compacted if it is trodden on again and again and this often happens at some key position adjacent to the paths. On the other hand some plants absolutely demand that you tread on the soil in order to work on top of them – for example, lifting parsnips or, even more so, scorzonera, where you have to dig down 15 inches (38cm) or so to lift the root. Then the larger brassicas (sprouts, winter cauliflower), anyway, prefer to be planted in a very firm, compacted soil that can only be achieved by standing on it and stamping it down. If they are not planted in firm soil they will certainly need staking or they will rock and eventually topple over; and staking is not too easy either if you have to reach over from a path two feet away. Of course, it is possible to make a platform of wood that arches over the

bed and which you can use to work from, but to be sturdy enough to last it must be strongly made; this means that it will be quite hefty and heavy, becoming a real nuisance to cart around the garden with you. But I suppose there is a mid-position which says: yes, all right, you do sometimes walk on your beds to lift this or that crop and to plant others, but you are careful not to do so when weeding and hoeing, you do not tramp over it to take short cuts, and you do not wheel your wheelbarrow over it. It is this sort of continual use that does the harm, and it is important to keep it down to a minimum.

Then, there is the problem of spacing of larger plants. The maximum size for a bed if you are to reach the centre from the sides is about 48 inches (122cm), unless, of course, you have exceptionally long arms or can afford to employ a robot (thank heavens no one has yet designed a robot gardener, but doubtless it will come!). This means that if you stick to a distance apart for your larger vegetables (for example, brussels sprouts) of 32 inches (80cm), and wish to fit in two rows, they will only be 8 inches (20cm) from the edge of the path, so that from about August onwards your paths will be blocked. It also means that about one-quarter to one-fifth of their root-run will be under the path where effective fertility will be nil. You could have the rows closer together, say 24 inches (60cm) apart and this would cut down the root-run under the path to less than one-tenth, but in that case you would have to space the plants wider apart in the rows. To give sprouts or sprouting broccoli sufficient space for growth you would have to plant them about 40 inches (100cm) apart in the rows, and this means that instead of fitting twelve plants in a 30 feet (9.15m) row you would only get about seven, or, at a pinch, nine.

An alternative would be to have narrower beds, say 3 feet (0.9m) wide, which would mean one row of large plants per bed. This would suit many people for whom the long stretch that 4 foot (1.2m) beds involve is a bit of an effort. But the trouble here is that if you have 3 foot (0.9m) beds with a 1 foot (30cm) path between them, then your rows are effectively 4 feet (1.2m) apart instead of 32 inches (80cm), and this again will reduce the number of plants you can grow per square foot by a third. It also means that although you would now have two spaces for intercropping between each row (one on each side of the path) these would be very close to the edge of the bed and you could only grow small crops there.

A third possibility, of course, is not to grow ordinary brussels sprouts, since it is now possible to grow dwarf ones whose normal spacing is 24 inches × 24 inches (60×60cm), and to grow smaller cauliflowers at the same distance, and to do the best you can with other plants that take up a lot of space, such as potatoes. But my own feeling is that the bed system is not economical for any crop that requires wide spacing; that is, potatoes, Jerusalem artichokes, or any of the large brassicas. For other crops, well, maybe . . . . I think this is a case of not proven either way, as far as maximum food production goes.

So, this is quite a difficult choice to make and very often the decision will be influenced, if not determined, by circumstances: for example, if your garden is such that other parts of it are already divided up into small beds you may think it simpler to garden it all by a bed system. If you only want to grow salad crops and small plants it is also worth trying. And if you really value the decorative effect of growing vegetables, you may decide that small beds do add a great deal. On the other hand, if you are really keen to grow the maximum crop of large brassicas, potatoes, etc., which are, after all, the mainstay of the vegetable garden, you are more likely to decide on the normal system. Similarly, if you have a large area and make use of rotovators and other mechanical tools, you are, I think, better off under the row system.

Of course, there is no reason why you should not divide your garden up, using the bed system for salad crops and some summer vegetables and the normal system for larger plants. This would make if difficult to get the most out of the space, however, and it would also present problems if you want to practise crop rotation. The bed system is still quite a rarity and so this book concentrates on the normal row system. However, a great deal of its advice applies equally to both systems.

Here, let me make a suggestion. When you take over a new garden, cultivate it on a temporary basis for the first year. There are two reasons for this. The first is that there may be all kinds of treasures, hidden at first sight, but later to be revealed to you in their due season. The second is that even the most experienced and confident gardener needs at least one season to get the feel of a new garden – how easy different parts of it are to dig and to work in, what is most convenient, how it looks, where the cold spots are, where the wind blows, where the cats run. This applies just as much to such decisions as where you put your compost heap, greenhouse, frame, garden shed, and even your paths. Of course you cannot mark time altogether, and some long-term decisions may be obvious, or inescapable. But it is unlikely that you will be able to get the whole plot into full production the first year, so try to concentrate on cultivating and improving the fertility of those parts of

Figure 7: Spacing of plants in 4 feet (1.3m) and 3 feet (1m) wide beds

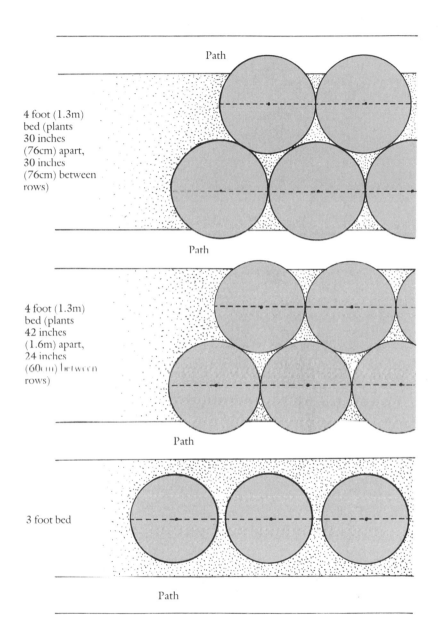

4 foot (1.3m)
bed (plants
30 inches
(76cm) apart,
30 inches
(76cm) between
rows)

4 foot (1.3m)
bed (plants
42 inches
(1.6m) apart,
24 inches
(60cm) between
rows)

3 foot bed

it that look as if they have previously had annual vegetables and which are not likely candidates for something (such as a swimming pool, or a tennis court) that will nullify the work you put in.

CHAPTER 3
THE CROPS

The next step is to decide what to grow – initially, of course, what you would like to grow. These preferences are likely to have to be modified by other factors – the type of soil, its fertility, the climate, the presence of diseases, the aspect, and so on.

In addition it will, of course, be determined by the size of your garden, and the amount of time you can afford to spend gardening, as well as your experience and skill. In selecting which vegetables to give priority you will be influenced naturally by your personal preferences but this is only one of the factors to be taken into account: to give an obvious example, most people like potatoes and probably eat more potatoes than any other vegetable – but this does not necessarily mean that they make a sensible crop for a small garden. What are the other factors that need to be thought of?

Freshness By the time shop vegetables have been picked, packaged, collected by or delivered to the wholesaler, stored, loaded into vans, delivered to the shops, displayed and eventually bought, several days or even weeks may have elapsed. This may not affect some vegetables all that much, but others by this time will have acquired a limpness, a curling and withering and yellowing of the edges, brown streaks at their hearts, a wrinkled dessication of their skins, a flaccid sadness about their whole aspect: this applies most of all to salad and green crops and it is they that are probably the most worthwhile to grow. Many other crops suffer almost as badly, and one is often faced with the dismal choice between gnarled parsnips that seem to consist of some strange rubbery fungus, and dry pallid carrots that no decent donkey would give a hee-haw for.

Unusual vegetables Vegetables do not have to be very unusual to be hard to obtain, because their availability outside London and big centres may still be very limited. To be sure, the situation is better than it used to be and you now see aubergines, peppers, garlic, chicory, and occasionally endive, even in small towns – but how often do you see salsify or celeriac or Batavian endive or any of the Italian chicories that Joy Larkcom has introduced into this country? For that matter, how often do you see a tomato other than Moneymaker or those giants such as Marmande which are described in the seed catalogues as being 'firm and fleshy' – a dauntingly accurate description?

However, I think it is worth issuing a word of warning about unusual vegetables. When, over forty years ago, Eleanour Sinclair Rohde's classic *Uncommon Vegetables and Fruits* was published one rather soured reviewer wrote: 'Eleanour Sinclair Rohde has done a service by calling attention to some excellent vegetables that have undeservedly fallen out of popular favour. In many cases however, there are very good reasons why the vegetables she extols are uncommon – and long may they remain so.' The same applies today. Some vegetables are unusual because they are unsuited to our climate, others because they are unsuited to the most generous palate. Below, I have tried to produce an unbiased seed list though, of course, all such assessments are coloured by the bias of personal preferences.

Expensive vegetables Asparagus, artichokes, aubergine .... Vegetables are expensive for all sort of reasons – because they take up a good deal of space or time, require a lot of labour, are imported, or because demand is very limited. It does not necessarily mean they are difficult to grow or beyond the resources of a small garden.

Easy-to-grow vegetables Busy people and beginners will not want to bother with vegetables that are difficult or that demand a lot of time. There is a distinction here between crops that are a lot of trouble such as, for example, peas which require sticking or netting, and then at the end of the season unsticking and un-netting, and those such as celery which, as well as being quite a lot of trouble, require considerable care and skill, and even then are often a disappointment.

Pollution Nearly all commercial vegetables are grown with the aid of pesticides, herbicides and chemical fertilizers and many people are rightly worried about the cumulative effect of this especially in relation to children.

Quality Even when vegetables are readily available (for example, peas and beans) the varieties on offer are very limited and are dictated by market considerations (shelf life, ease of packaging, appearance, productivity, etc.) rather than by quality.

I think it is worth listing all the vegetables you might think of growing and assessing them from the point of view of the above considerations. You will, of course, probably consult and compare several seed catalogues. But quite often the superlatives in which these are couched are a hindrance to making sensible choices rather than a help. So what I am going to attempt is to produce what is effectively a basic seed catalogue shorn of the sales talk, though, of course, my preferences will be personal and I cannot claim that they are totally objective.

Chinese artichoke This is about the only vegetable in the list that I have never grown; I cannot think why because both Jane Grigson and Joy Larkcom agree that 'these are easy to grow, easy to cook and exceptionally delicious to eat.' The only reservation is that the tiniest tubers left in the ground will re-sprout and, like their namesakes (but no relative) Jerusalem artichokes, they can become invasive. The other snag is that they are difficult to get hold of, but apart from that I can give no first-hand advice about them.

Globe artichoke A very large perennial with handsome foliage and flowers which can better be grown in the flower border. In France it is a crop of commercial importance and some French growers go to great lengths to maximize their crops, but in Britain we just let it grow with very little trouble except to protect it from frosts in very cold areas and to manure and water it copiously. It is better to propagate by suckers than by seed, which does not always breed true. Grand Vert de Camus is the best variety if you can get hold of it.

Jerusalem artichoke A very easy crop to grow, very nutritious, will produce a crop in quite poor soil, and provides an excellent windbreak. It is fairly difficult to find in shops. It has a slightly earthy flavour which is not to everyone's taste and it should not be indulged in too often, at any rate until you have established the family reaction to it. But cream of artichoke and potato soup is one of the very best vegetable soups, so it is a crop I never want to be without.

Asparagus A luxury crop, though it is not too difficult to grow. It is a supreme vegetable with the advantage that it crops in June when there are very few other vegetables to be harvested. But plants are expensive to buy and it takes three or four years to produce a reasonable crop from seed. Asparagus can be grown either in a permanent bed, or in rows in succession – in both cases it takes up a lot of space. The best variety is probably Evesham Giant.

Aubergine Normally a greenhouse crop (which is outside the area of this book), aubergines can only be grown out of doors in a very warm sunny spot and even then you will not have a large crop. Only tackle aubergines if you like a challenge and are prepared for the possibility of disappointment.

Broad bean The best crop (though probably not the tastiest) is the autumn-sown one that brings the first 'summer vegetables' in early June, avoids blackfly damage, and occupies space through the winter which would otherwise be empty. They are easy to grow, though there is a danger from mice eating the seed as soon as you sow it, from the seed rotting before it germinates if the weather becomes very cold and wet, and from frost if the plant has been allowed to grow too high in the autumn (in a mild autumn you should defer sowing till late November). It is best to pre-germinate the seed or sow in boxes

– so, although once growing they are very little trouble, they are like the old 6-volt Renault – a bit of a problem to get started. Sow the variety Aquadulce.

Dwarf French bean A simple and excellent crop to grow and there are many excellent varieties you cannot usually buy in the shops. Try the varieties Tendergreen and Sprite.

Climbing French bean and runner bean Since bean poles are hard to obtain and bamboos costly to buy there is a problem in supporting them – but runner beans are a must for every gardener, and nearly everyone grows far more than they can eat or pick – to the detriment of the crop. There are some excellent varieties, such as the French bean Blue Lake, which are far tastier and far less inclined to be stringy than the old favourites, though some of them are F_1 hybrids which are expensive and whose seeds cannot be saved for the next year's crop.

Beetroot An easy crop, though in the north they have to be lifted and stored for the winter. An advantage of home-grown beet is that you can eat the leaves as well – an excellent vegetable that you never see in the shops. Grow Boltardy for summer crops, and Forono for main crops.

Broccoli, Sprouting This is a vegetable that has recently begun to appear in the shops though the green type (known as calabrese) is expensive and the late white sprouting type (an April/May crop) is never to be seen. Sprouting broccoli is one of the large brassicas that need a lot of space and a good rich soil. It occupies the ground for nearly twelve months – but then rewards you with an abundant crop between March and May. *Calabrese* is a quick-growing late summer and autumn crop that can follow early summer vegetables for a late autumn crop.

Brussels sprouts Another marathon crop, planted out in May or June and in some cases still going strong the following April. It is not easy to grow well, often producing a majority of open 'blown' heads – though these need not be wasted as they are useful for winter salads. Brussels sprouts must have a rich soil and be very firmly planted and if grown in an open or windy site will need to be staked or substantially earthed up for support.

Cabbage You can grow cabbages for harvesting in every month of the year – but who wants to? They are a useful crop for the winter, but spring cabbage seems to me to be the most useful. *Chinese cabbage* grows very quickly and can follow summer crops. They are an excellent salad vegetable and are not too difficult to grow though it is not easy to match cabbages grown commercially in tunnels.

Cardoon A plant similar in size and appearance to the globe artichoke and perhaps also best grown in the flower garden. The stalks are blanched in a similar way to celery. Almost never to be seen in the shops. I know of only one place where you can get seed in Britain, and that is the Henry Doubleday Research Association at Ryton on Dunsmore, Coventry. You may have to use artichoke stalks, which make a reasonable substitute for this vegetable.

Carrot If your soil is clayey or stony, carrots are difficult to grow well. If it is sandy or silty they are easier but there may be problems with carrot fly, which is very difficult to control and whose larvae – little white grubs – can devastate a crop. But it is worth trying to grow carrots because commercial crops are kept free from carrot fly with powerful pesticides, and carrots more than any other plant have an unfortunate tendency to absorb and retain these. Shop carrots are, therefore, one of the vegetables most under suspicion from a health point of view.

Cauliflower Winter cauliflowers are often a disappointment. They need a long growth period, rich soil and firm planting, without which they give poor results. Also, when they do crop they do so all at once, so you really need to sow a number of different varieties to mature at different times. All the same they are one of the most satisfying crops to grow well, especially the late ones that mature in May and even very early June when good vegetables are at a premium. In sheltered areas the old-fashioned varieties Winter White, Early March, May Queen, etc., will survive all but the hardest winters, but for cold areas the Walcheren varieties, or a purple-headed type such as Purple Cape, as safer – they even survived the winter of 1984/85.

Celery Winter celery is a difficult crop to grow well. Although it is usually tastier than the shop variety it seldom matches its crispness and cleanness. Growing celery from seed is tricky and is liable to produce plants that bolt. Earthing it up and at the same time protecting it from mud, worms and slugs is also a problem. The autumn self-blanching variety is a different matter altogether, but it is only worth growing if you can provide it with a very rich soil and keep it watered regularly.

Celeriac Rare in the shops, celeriac is an excellent vegetable and is not nearly so difficult to grow as celery, though it also requires a rich soil. Unfortunately, plants for planting out are hard to come by and growing your own from seed is a bit tricky. The seed is very fine and according to most books has to be sown in heat. This is not necessary if you pre-germinate the seed and I have described how to do this in Chapter 5.

Celtuce A plant very similar to lettuce in both its growth and its use in salads.

Chicory The chicory you buy in the shops are chicons produced by forcing Witloof Chicory. They are all imported and they are nothing like so good as home-grown ones. These are not difficult to produce though, as with all forcing, it is quite a time-consuming process.

There are many other chicories, none of which are ever available in the shops, and if you are a green salad addict they are a must. It is difficult to find the seed of many of these but the HDRA stock several and a few seedsmen market Sugar-loaf for summer and Rosso for winter.

Claytonia (Winter Purslane) This has small soft, flavourless leaves which, I must confess, do not fill me with enthusiasm. It can be used as a summer salad and is also useful for winter though it is said not to survive a hard frost.

Coriander Is familiar in many kitchens as a seed but is widely used as a green crop in Indian cooking. It has a strong flavour similar to the seed but more aromatic. It is easy to grow in the summer and the seed you buy in Indian shops is cheaper than that from seed merchants and is usually quite reliable as regards germination.

Corn salad An easy-to-grow winter salad.

Land cress (sometimes called *American Cress*) Another easy winter salad very worth growing. It is not quite so succulent as watercress, which it closely resembles, but it makes a very good substitute, and it will survive the hardest frost.

Cucumbers Again I am only concerned with outdoor cucumbers. Those old coarse spongy cucumbers we grew in the past can now be relegated to the limbo of forgotten things as there are improved outdoor varieties – though they are not, in my experience, quite so prolific as the seed catalogues claim! But they are reasonably easy to grow, though they need careful watering (there is a danger of over-watering) and it is usually necessary to hand-pollinate them. Both lemon and apple cucumber are worth a try: they produce a lot of small cucumbers with the shape, but not the taste, of apple (or lemon).

Dandelion Much used in France, but hardly at all in Britain. You can buy seeds of the cultivated kind or, alternatively, keep your eyes open in the country and take a root cutting from any that have large healthy leaves. It is usual to blanch the leaves as they are very bitter unblanched – though a few of the unblanched leaves can add a pleasant 'bite' to a green salad.

Endive You grow these just like lettuces except that you need to bunch the leaves together and tie them up three or four weeks before use, preferably on a fine, dry day. If you do not do this the leaves are bitter – but even so they can make a pleasant addition to a salad in small quantities. Their main problem is that if they get wet when they are bunched up they go brown and decay. This seems particularly likely to happen if they are covered over with a bucket or box for blanching (as is often recommended) so I much prefer to tie them. There are two kinds. There is the curly-headed, of which I grow Riccia di Pancalieri which will survive quite hard frosts (even if the outer leaves suffer, they protect the heart which remains untouched so long as they have been well tied up); I think this is probably the same variety as is sold by the HDRA as Endiva Riccia. The other kind is the Batavian, of which there are several varieties, though British seed merchants only seem to stock one, which is unnamed. It is an extremely good crisp salad vegetable almost never seen in British shops and not very often in British gardens, nor for that matter in British seed catalogues.

Another advantage of endive is that slugs and snails do not seem to like it much. In fact, endive make a very trouble-free crop except for the small chore of tying them up for blanching, and I cannot think why people do not grow them more.

Fennel, sweet (Finocchio) This is a biennial and is different from the herb fennel which is a perennial. It is seldom grown in this country, and certainly it is not possible to achieve the very large bulbs that can be grown in Mediterranean countries. But huge bulbs are not essential, or even necessarily an advantage, and the bulbs it does produce are full of flavour and all the better for being picked fresh. It is one of the very best vegetables, but the difficulty with it is its tendency to bolt to seed instead of producing bulbs. This seems to happen when it comes to maturity in the hot dry summer months, so I think that the instructions nearly always given to sow it in the spring are wrong. Try sowing it in July for a September crop. In Italy they transplant it in September/October for a spring crop, but it will not survive hard frosts. However, it is worth trying this if you can give it some protection. Apart from the problem of bolting fennel is not difficult to grow. It is a beautiful plant and the leaves are useful for flower decorations as well as for flavouring.

Garlic The wrong instructions are usually given here, too. Garlic should be planted in the late autumn as shallots used to be. If you plant it in the spring it does not have time to develop enough growth by midsummer when it ceases new growth and concentrates its energies on bulb (or, more accurately, clove) production. It is essential, therefore, to grow a hardy kind; that is, the larger cloves, preferably those tinted red or purple, which can be bought from Indian shops and some greengrocers rather than the small Mediterranean ones you get from grocers. Cloves bought in shops seem quite satisfactory and there is no need to buy expensive ones from seed merchants. Like onions, garlic needs a rich soil and the only problem in growing it occurs at planting time. Frosts will lift the cloves from the ground, but they also lift themselves out, raising themselves on their own roots. So, before planting, it is important to loosen the soil to a depth of 3 or 4 inches (7.5–10cm) and then firm the cloves in from the top when you are planting them. Another snag is that once they have spotted them the birds (mainly blackbirds) will come and peck at them, and having discovered they do not like them will toss them on one side. Unfortunately, they do not learn very quickly from experience and it is not unusual for one bird to peck its way right down a row scattering cloves as it goes, and still not get the message. You need to check up on this at least twice a week, firmly replacing the victims until they are well-rooted. Alternatively, as I do, start them off in pots in the spare bedroom and then plant them out.

Good King Henry Another useful spring salading, easy to grow. It is a perennial and the shoots are picked like asparagus.

Kale There are many kales, some of which are extremely hardy. It is worth growing a few plants in case we have a really hard winter which decimates other crops. The type most usually grown is curly kale, often known as borecole, which you sometimes find in shops. It is worth trying other kinds such as asparagus kale and thousand-headed, but you will have to search for the seed as it is getting quite difficult to find any variety other than curly kale.

Kohlrabi An alternative to and, many think, an improvement on turnips, which have the advantage that they can be transplanted. There is a purple variety and a green one. I have never felt there was much difference in flavour, but the purple one looks more interesting and dramatic.

Leek Easy to grow, and invaluable.

Lettuce Commercial lettuce production is geared to survival under market conditions, which limits it to two or three varieties. There are many different lettuces, and they are all quite easy to grow though you have to be prepared to grapple with the problem of slugs. Most people sow too many in the spring and too few at other times. Lobjots and Little Gem are both small crisp lettuces that take up little room and are suitable for inter-cropping and also for producing 'leaf lettuce'. Valdor is good for overwintering. Buttercrunch makes small, tender but crisp hearts, Minett is a small crisp head, and if you want a large lettuce Webbs Wonderful is still hard to beat. But it is a good idea to try at least one new variety each year until you find your favourites.

Marrow and courgette By buying early varieties, starting these off in your spare bedroom and taking some trouble with pollination, you can produce a lot of courgettes when the price in the shops is high, and this is well worth it.

Whether growing marrows justifies the space they take depends on how much space you have available and how much you like them.

Nasturtium Usually grown for its flowers, but this is a salad vegetable that I definitely would recommend. Its leaves have a unique peppery flavour, its flowers are edible and make a colourful addition to any salad, and can also, like marrow flowers, be cooked in batter (similar to Japanese tempura). In addition, the seeds can be pickled to make a very good alternative to capers. If you grown one of the compact varieties it will make a colourful border to the vegetable or salad garden.

Onions Now that a wider range of sets is available, these are preferable to seeds except for the specialist or enthusiast. Autumn-sown Japanese onions (again preferably sets which can be sown as late as October, or even in a mild November) to mature the following June or early July, are definitely worth a trial.

Parsley Most people are agreed that French parsley has the better flavour, but it is not completely hardy and goes to seed rather early in the spring. So it is worth sowing French in the spring and the more usual moss-curled in the late summer to stand the winter.

Parsley, Hamburg As well as parsley-like leaves this produces a parsnip-like root. It is easy to grow, and both leaves and root are good to eat.

Orach A mild and rather boring salad crop whose main attraction is that its leaves are red and add a welcome touch of colour to salads. There is also a green variety but the red is far preferable: it grows quite tall and is attractive enough to be grown in the flower border.

Parsnip Easy to grow. Seed sown in

April or May will produce smaller, cleaner roots.

Peas Like beans, shops have a very limited selection on sale. If you want French petit-pois, sugar- or snap-peas, or asparagus peas you will probably have to grow them yourself. The snag with peas is that most of the best ones need supporting with sticks or netting. If you live in town twiggy sticks are quite hard to come by; plastic netting is cheap and will last for ages but disentangling it all at the end of each season is a real bind, and so is folding it neatly away for the winter in a way that can be unwound easily again the following summer. But it is worth it because peas fresh from the garden are one of the most joyous rewards of gardening.

Peppers Can be grown out of doors in a very sheltered sunny spot. You will not have a big crop and most of them will probably have to be picked green, but for salads fresh peppers from the garden are tasty enough to be worth it. Plants are not all that difficult to come by nowadays and they are not too difficult to raise from seed in a similar way to tomatoes. But this is only a crop for people who are prepared to take quite a bit of trouble.

Potatoes Not too difficult to grow, though rather susceptible to pests and diseases (blight which can be controlled, eelworm which cannot). I think it is worth taking some risk to get really early new potatoes – I have more doubts about the value of growing your own maincrop, especially now that one of the best of all maincrops, Desirée, is available everywhere (though it is worth mentioning that the potato is one of the crops where the flavour and quality of home-grown chemical-free vegetables is very noticeably superior to the shop produce). Try several varieties

over the years but I suggest Maris Bard or Duke of York for earlies and Desirée or Record for maincrop.

Pumpkin Easy to grow, but they need a lot of feeding, space and water. It is quite possible to grow pumpkins that weigh a hundredweight but I do not know what you do with them when you have grown them. There are many varieties – the HDRA stocks several seeds.

Radish Sow a few at a time and pick when young – except the Chinese and Japanese types which grow very large. The winter varieties Black Spanish and China Rose are easy to grow, and are a valuable addition to winter salads.

Rhubarb Most people stick with rhubarb they have inherited or been given. As the crop lasts indefinitely it is worth starting out with a good variety that crops early such as Timperly Early; this is a trouble-free crop.

Rocket (sometimes called *Arugula*) This salad vegetable is very popular in Italy, but hardly grown in Britain. It is a very small plant, but the leaves have a distinctive flavour so you do not need much of it. It tends to go to seed, but you can go on using the leaves so long as it goes on producing them (they get stronger and sharper in flavour though). If left to go to seed it will propagate itself. Not everyone enjoys its strong distinctive flavour, but it is definitely worth trying.

Salsify and *Scorzonera* Two rather similar vegetables with a delicate flavour which you can very seldom buy in the shops. They are a bit of trouble to grow, especially in clayey or stony soils, in which case it may be necessary to make a conical hole which you can fill with fine compost for them to grow in. Also, lifting them can be quite a problem, especially in the case of scorzonera which grows to a depth of 18 inches (45cm) or more. The seeds do not germinate very well and it would be nice to sow them quite thickly, but this could be expensive as there are very few seeds in a packet (only 15 in a packet from one very well-known seedsman). It is easy to save seed, though, and the plants produce very beautiful seedheads.

Seakale This is an epicurean vegetable which is almost unobtainable now. It takes two or three years to produce its first crop of blanched stems, which it will continue to produce for about five years. So, it needs to be sown in or transplanted to a permanent bed well supplied with compost and probably with lime as it will not thrive in an acid soil. It is not difficult to grow but, of course, all plants that require blanching need quite a bit of attention.

Shallot Milder and smaller than onions, shallots have the advantage that they can be harvested in July. They are easy to grow. The traditional date for planting is 22 December (the shortest day), but follow the seedsman's instructions as most modern varieties are bred for spring planting. The smaller bulbs can be saved from one year to plant for the next.

Sorrel Sorrel is a perennial that will last for ages and needs little attention. Cut off the seedheads when they appear in summer and also the coarse outer leaves from time to time to stimulate the growth of new tender leaves from the centre. Sorrel is useful for salads and also for the creation of sour-sweet flavours. In fact sour-sweet is not the sole invention of the Chinese – it occurs in the traditional Cornish recipe 'squab pie' where lamb chops are flavoured with apple, onion and sorrel – in this case the wild sorrel which grows abundantly in Cornish hedgerows. It is very good, too, as a flavouring with spinach, especially in lasagne. Cultivated sorrel is the French variety which has larger leaves and a less sharp tang to it. It is worth trying to get some plants of the wild kind as well if you have a chance. *The Book of Rarer Vegetables* by George Wythers and Harry Roberts, published in the 'twenties (at 15p for the hardback edition!), mentions a dozen varieties of sorrel but I do not think it is possible to obtain seed for more than two or three of them nowadays, except perhaps in France.

Spinach An easy vegetable to grow for summer or winter, except that the summer variety bolts in hot weather, so do not grow too much at a time.

Spinach beet This is an excellent trouble-free winter or summer vegetable. It can be sown *in situ* as late as August, or planted out in early September, following summer vegetables, for a winter crop.

Seakale beet (Swiss chard) Very worth while growing, this lasts longer than spinach beet before going to seed. If planted 12 inches (30cm) apart in rich deep soil it can produce tender succulent leaves and stalks up to 2 feet (0.6m) long.

Ruby chard This looks attractive but turns green when cooked and tastes much the same as Swiss chard. It is not quite so hardy either and may not survive the winter.

New Zealand spinach This is a summer spinach only as it is not at all hardy. Its only advantage is that it will tolerate hot, dry weather without bolting, but it is very definitely not a vegetable for the gourmet.

Swede Alas, the old rich-flavoured orange swedes that I remember from my childhood seem to have disappeared for ever and the offering now is a kind of large, rather mild, insipid turnip. But swedes are very hardy and perhaps it is worth growing a few.

Sweet corn The best hybrids have very sweet cobs, far superior to any you buy in the shops. But these often only produce one or two cobs per plant; the seed is expensive and cannot be saved for next year as it does not breed true. All the same it is a delicious vegetable and worth growing.

Tomato About the only plants you can buy in most places are Moneymaker, Alicante and Outdoor Girl. If you want other varieties you will probably have to grow them from seed yourself. This is not too difficult and you do not need a heated greenhouse or a propagator if you pre-germinate the seeds. But it is time-consuming and you have to be around to see to the watering. The old varieties Harbinger and Ailsa Craig have good flavour. Some of the small-fruited ones such as Gardeners Delight have very sweet fruit. If you want an early crop there are several F1 hybrids such as Gemini. Personally, I am not very partial to the large 'meaty' varieties such as Marmande but they are worth growing if you like cooked or stuffed tomatoes.

Turnip Has the advantage that seed for the winter crop can be sown late (July–August) and so it can follow summer crops. This is important if you are practising a rotation as turnips are brassicas (cabbage family) and space for them is limited.

Figure 8 lists all the above crops and provides some rough and ready information about them.

Freshness: ● home-grown, fresh-picked produce is much superior to shop produce (mostly salad crops).

Unusual: ● only available in classy or enterprising shops, and in many cases not at all.
●● usually only obtainable in big towns, or at some Indian shops or enterprising market stalls.
●●● almost never obtainable.

Expensive: refers to price of produce in shops.
● usually expensive.
●● always expensive.
E expensive when early, but may not be so otherwise.
− it is hard to price vegetables that are virtually unobtainable.

Quality: ● although easily obtainable, if you want the best quality varieties you probably have to grow them yourself.

Easy: ●● no problems.
● needs care and/or attention, but not really difficult.
D difficult.

Soil: ● does not need a very rich soil to produce a reasonable crop.
S easy in a sandy or coarse, silty soil, less so otherwise

Swiss chard (or seakale beet), Hamburg parsley and fennel.

Kohlrabi is a member of the brassica family and has a delicate turnip taste.

Globe artichokes are spectacular vegetables. Grand Vert de Camus is the best variety to grow if you can find it.

Figure 8: A summary of crops you can grow

	Freshness	Unusual	Expensive	Quality	Easy	Soil	Remarks
Chinese artichoke		●●●	–		?	?	I have never grown it
Globe artichoke		●●	●●		●●		
Jerusalem artichoke		●	●		●●	●	
Asparagus	●		●●		●		
Aubergine		●	●		D		difficult to get a crop without glass
Broad beans	●		E		●	●	
Dwarf beans	●		E	●	●		
Climbing beans	●		E	●	●		
Runner beans	●		E		●		
Beetroot					●●	●	
Broccoli		●			●		
Brussel sprouts					●		
Cabbage					●●	●	
Cardoon	–	●●●	–		●		
Carrots					●	S	Carrot-root-fly nearly always a problem
Cauliflower					●		
Celeriac	–	●	●		D		difficult to grow from seed
Celery					D		ditto, and also hard to blanch
Celtuce	●	●●●	–		●●	●	
Chicory chicons	●	●	●		●	●	
Chicory	●	●●●	–		●●	●	
Claytonia	–	●●●	–		●●	●	
Coriander	–	●			●●	●	obtainable from Indian shops
Corn salad	–	●●●	–		●●	●	
Cress (land)	–	●●●	–		●●	●	
Cucumber					●		
Dandelion		●●●	–		●●	●	
Endive	●	●●	●		●●	●	
Finocchio	●	●●	●●		●		difficult to stop it bolting in summer
Garlic					●		

	Freshness	Unusual	Expensive	Quality	Easy	Soil	Remarks
Good King Henry	–	●●●	–		●●	●	
Kale		●		●	●●	●	
Kohlrabi		●●	●		●●	●	
Leek					●●	●	
Lettuce	●			●	●●	●	
Marrow/courgette					●		
Nasturtium	–	●●●	–		●●	●	grow in poor soil if you want flowers
New Zealand spinach		●●●	–		●●	●	
Onions					●		
Parsley	●				●	●	
Parsley (Hamburg)	–	●●●	–		●●	S	
Orach	–	●●●	–		●●	●	
Parsnip					●●	S	
Peas	●		E	●	●		
Peppers	●				D	●	only a very warm sheltered spot will give you a crop
Potatoes			E	●	●●		
Pumpkin		●●			●		
Radish	●				●●	●	
Rhubarb			E		●●	●	
Rocket	–	●●●	–		●●	●	
Salsify	–	●●	●		●	S	
Scorzonera	–	●●●	–		●	S	
Seakale	–	●●●	–		D		
Shallots					●●		
Sorrel	–	●●●	–		●●	●	must be one of the easiest crops, it just goes on growing
Spinach	●	●			●	●	
Spinach beet	●	●			●●	●	
Seakale beet	–	●●			●●	●	
Swede					●●	●	
Sweet corn				●	●		
Tomatoes			E	●	●	●	
Turnip					●●	●	

CHAPTER 4
SIMPLE PLANNING

Having pored over the list of vegetables and over the seed catalogues, you then compile your own list of what you want to grow. You must make sure that this can be accommodated in the space you have available, and if it cannot then you must pare it down until it can. This is not just a matter of dividing the space taken by each crop into the total space you have available because, of course, some crops overlap or coincide and others do not. In addition, some take a very long time to grow and others are in and out of the ground before you can say 'Jill Robinson'. Also, some eventually take up a great deal of space. In particular, many of the crops you grow for the winter will also have to be growing in their allotted place during much of the summer; in fact, some crops such as sprouts and late winter cauliflowers may well remain in position for almost the whole of the twelve months. For this reason – which will be elaborated upon as we go along – it is mainly these long-growing vegetables that are the key to our planning, and it is these that we will consider first. Over the page, in Table 1, is a list of the main winter crops and the date by which they are normally sown or planted in position.

Opinions differ about the optimum date for planting and sowing and I have here taken an average viewpoint. It is generally agreed that for leeks, sprouts, broccoli and cauliflower, an early planting is advisable, though I will explain here why I have reservations about these generally accepted dates.

You will see from the above list that only a few of the winter vegetables are normally sown or planted out later than July, and many need to be in their permanent quarters earlier than this. Equally, only a few very early summer crops are out of the ground *before* July, so obviously there is a clash of interest here: those that will not be ready obviously cannot occupy rows that are earmarked for winter vegetables. It is this overlapping that creates problems for gardeners. Clearly you must either leave space vacant throughout the early summer; or, if you do not, by the time your summer vegetables are harvested it is too late to plant your winter vegetables and the ground will remain vacant throughout the winter. Alternatively there will be a great overcrowding during the late summer to the detriment both of the plants that are due for harvesting and those that you are just planting. The results of each of these possibilities are a common sight in allotments and gardens, and account for much of the overcrowding, undercropping and wasted space that good planning tries to avoid.

The best solution to this problem is to interplant the majority of your summer vegetables between the rows where the winter vegetables are or will be, so that your summer crops are coming to maturity just when your

Table 1: When to sow or plant main winter crops

Brassicas		
Brassicas (the cabbage family)	Brussels sprouts	May/June ⎫
	Sprouting broccoli	June/July ⎪ Planted out
	Winter cauliflower	June/July ⎬ from seedbed.
	Cabbage, etc.	June/July ⎭
	Kale	June/July Planted out or sown *in situ*.
	Swede	June ⎫ Sown *in situ*.
	Turnip	July/August ⎬
	Spring cabbage	September/October Planted out.
Root crops	Parsnip	March/April, but can be sown in May.
	Salsify	April/May
	Scorzonera	April/May
	Carrot	June/July
	Beetroot	June/July
Onion crops	Onion	March
	Leek	May/June Planted out.
	Japanese onion	October (sets)
	Garlic	November (cloves)
	Shallot	December/Spring
Others	Celeriac ⎫ Celery ⎭	June/July Planted out.
	Spinach beet	
	Seakale beet (Swiss chard)	Sow late July or plant out August for consumption over winter and next spring.
	Ruby or Rhubarb chard	
	Broad beans ⎫ Hardy peas ⎭	November/December for harvesting next May/June.

winter crops are young and need less space, and so that as your winter crops grow and need progressively more space your summer ones will be harvested and lifted out of the way. If you can imagine the progress of two such rows throughout the summer, you will have the general pattern in Figure 9.

Although your main rows will be empty when you come to plant out your winter crops, and although your winter plants will be quite small, it is important to ensure that they are not overshadowed by the summer crops intercropped between them. So it is necessary to be very careful where you plant large lettuces, such as Salad Bowl or Webbs, or dwarf beans, or any other plant that might trespass on their space.

This obviously means that a number of large summer crops such as climbing peas, climbing beans, marrows and sweet corn cannot be intercropped but will have to occupy main rows.

To make room for this intercropping, your main winter rows will have to be spaced quite far apart. There is some choice in the distance between them depending on the size of your garden, the number of people you have to feed, your own preference, what crops you grow, and whether you prefer to use imperial or metric measurements. I started this system with rows 30 inches apart because I thought 36 inches was too wide for my small garden. But I have found 30 inches a bit crowded for sprouts, broccoli, etc. – not so much from the point of view of their growth, but for getting at them (for example, in a rather windy site they often need staking or earthing up), so now I use metric measurements and have changed to 80cm (just under 32 inches). It is surprising what a difference that 2 inches makes. But this distance apart of 80cm will, I am sure, alarm some people because it looks so wide. They may agree that the large brassicas (sprouts, cauliflowers, etc.) require this amount of space, but will feel that in the case of most of the other winter crops a lot of space will be wasted.

However, as you will see from the list on pages 33–34 there are a great number of small winter vegetables which you can use to intercrop between these rows. In any case, I think if you compare your garden with those of your neighbours you will find that this system does actually make fuller use of the space available.

To provide further justification, I am now going to anticipate later chapters and reveal that one of the main reasons for having this fixed distance between the rows is that it enables you to keep your rows in exactly the same position year after year. Obviously if one year you are growing sprouts in rows 2½ feet (77cm) apart and the next year you are growing parsnips in rows 18 inches (45cm) apart, the position of your rows is bound to vary from year to year. The advantage of having fixed permanent rows is principally this: the majority of your winter crops are heavy feeders and deep-rooting; thus they require different, and much deeper, cultivation and much heavier manuring than do most of the short-lived, shallow-rooted summer crops. Thus, by concentrating your winter crops within the limited areas of these rows, you are economizing on the amount of cultivation and, in particular, on the amount of organic fertilizer you have to apply. In addition, by keeping to the same rows year after year, you considerably simplify the process of planning and keeping records. Both of these aspects will be given their due attention in later chapters, but for the moment I ask you to take this distance and these fixed rows on trust.

Having decided on the distance

Figure 9: Interplanting summer crops between rows of winter vegetables

	→ Spring →	Early summer →	Midsummer →	Late summer →	Autumn →
Row 1	sow very early summer veg possibly under cloches ⟶	harvest these	e m p t y	plant out or sow winter veg	winter veg growing larger	winter veg take over
Inter-crop row	sow summer veg	summer veg growing ⟶		summer veg harvested		empty
Row 2	over-wintered crops (e.g. spring cabbage)	harvest these	e m p t y	plant out or sow winter veg	winter veg growing larger	winter veg take over

between rows there is every hope that you will not have to change it in the future, though I suggest that you wait until the second year of your occupancy to initiate this long-term planning system. In fact, even after that you may well find that your plans have not worked out exactly as you had calculated and you may have to change it. But, if all is well and there are no snags, you should be able to stick to this distance, and you should aim to do so. Throughout this book I am going to assume that we have decided on a distance apart of 80cm, but this is merely for convenience. The same principles apply whatever measurement you decide upon.

So, now we have one fixed measurement and it is a good idea to underwrite this by making a fixed measuring rod which you can use for all purposes. Once you have this you can forget the actual measurements between the rows altogether. Cut a wooden batten of 4–6cm (1–2 inches) square section the appropriate length (in our case 80cm) and then mark off the halves, quarters and eighths position with saw-cuts. Paint this an unmistakable (and unloseable) colour and you can use it for all your measuring. The advantage of the 80cm unit here is that it divides easily into 10cm lengths which you can use for measuring the distance between plants of 4 inches (10cm), 8 inches (20cm) or 12 inches (30cm). These measurements are convenient for most plants, especially since we now know that closer spacing is usually more productive than some of the older recommended distances.

Armed with this universal measuring rod you can now turn to your garden and see how your rows will fit in. Initially I am going to assume that the piece of land or allotment is a rectangular area 30 feet (9.15m) wide by 45 feet (13.2m). I am also going to assume that just under a third of this is taken up by a compost heap, a shed, and some permanent crops, leaving you an area 30 feet (9.15m) wide by 31 feet (9.5m). If each row occupies 80cm, this will enable you to fit in twelve rows (obtained by dividing the length 9.5m or 950cm by 80cm). This assumes that you run your rows across your allotment which, as you will observe, is what nearly all allotment holders do. If for some reason you decide you want to have your rows lengthways, then divide the width (9.15m) by 80cm giving you 11.4 – that is eleven rows of 9.5m (31 feet). This would give you some extra space at one end (or both ends) for intercropping, but not enough to fit in another main row. If you still want your twelve rows you would have to cut down the distance between the rows to 30 inches (77cm).

Perhaps this is the right moment to consider briefly which is the best way for the rows to run. For many years, repeated by rote in nearly every gardening book, we have been told that it is better to align your rows north/south rather than east/west. Nowadays many of the old rules of thumb are being questioned (ploughing, deep digging, planting dates, planting distances, etc.) and I think it is time this 'rule', too, was subjected to scrutiny. The theory appears to be that in this way your plants receive more light and more direct sunshine; thus they are able to effect more photosynthesis, and therefore grow better. Is this really so? Current practice is to grow vegetables at a distance much closer together in the rows than between the rows (e.g. turnips, carrots, etc., 2 inches (5cm) or 3 inches (7.5cm) apart in the rows, with rows 8 inches (20cm) or 10 inches (25cm) apart) so that if your row is aligned to the midday sun, when the light is at its brightest, the whole of the bottom of the plant will be in shade from the next plant in the row, and only the top leaves will be reached by the sun. If they are aligned east/west the space between the rows will allow the sun to slant down to the lower leaves, thus increasing the area exposed to light. But if we follow the new trend and grow our vegetables equidistant from each other in a triangular pattern, it does not really make any difference how they relate to the sun; they will receive the same amount of light however they are positioned. However, there is another point to consider in aligning your rows and that is shelter. As I have already mentioned, it is the cold northerly or north-easter which is the most detrimental to plants, and if you have a choice it is probably better to align your rows so that the wind does not blow straight down on them from this direction. The several allotment-holders I have talked to about this have scratched their heads and pointed out that regardless of sun and wind nearly all allotments are aligned across the width of the allotment, never mind what direction that is. So, this is a question that is not proven, and you should do whatever you prefer or is most convenient for you.

I think that for most families 30 feet (9.15m) rows are inconveniently long and I suggest we regard each full row as divided into two 15 foot (4.5m) rows. You could, if you like, make a path up the centre dividing these two halves; but this could be a waste of space since each row is easily accessible from the paths on either side of the allotment. So, what we now have is illustrated in Figure 10a and b.

Since it is intended that these positions for your rows should be permanent I suggest you mark them in some permanent way. To do this, obtain further lengths of 1 inch or 1½ inches (or thereabouts) section wood – 2.5 –4cm. Cut this into lengths of about 24 inches (60cm). It is quite an advantage if this is a good hardwood which will last and it is surprising how easy it is to come across this if you keep a weather eye open on dustbin day or on builders' skips (it is very expensive to buy). Broken deck chairs, cast-off children's play pens, clothes-drying frames, etc., all provide just the sort of wood you need; alternatively, 1 or 1½ inch iron pipe is also ideal. Every day huge quantities of such valuable materials are thrown away (much of it, of course, organic in origin and crying out for recycling in compost heaps – but that is another story!). Having cut your wood into lengths paint the top 6 inches (15cm) or so a colour according to your preference (in my case bright red, because I like to see clearly where things are) and the rest with a preservative (bituminous paint, for example). Then mark off your rows and hammer your battens or pipes into the ground at the end of each row. Knock them in quite lightly to start with, until you feel sure that you have them positioned exactly how you want them. Then hammer them in very firmly so that only the top 6 inches (15cm) is showing. These will be permanent markers for your winter rows, and will remain there indefinitely, so it is worth taking quite a bit of trouble to get them accurate, firm and clearly visible. You might find it helpful to number each of your rows and to paint the number on the appropriate marker; this will simplify your planning and guard against any danger of confusion.

While you are doing this it is also a good idea to measure the length of your rows. If you have an allotment or a rectangular patch your rows will all be

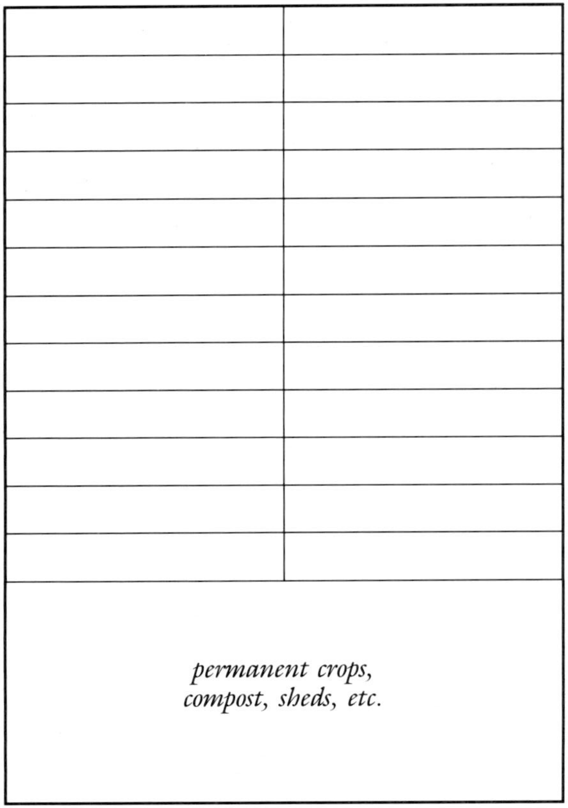

Figure 10b: Rows along the length of your allotment or garden
24 rows each 4.75 m long, 76 cm apart (16 ft × 30 in)

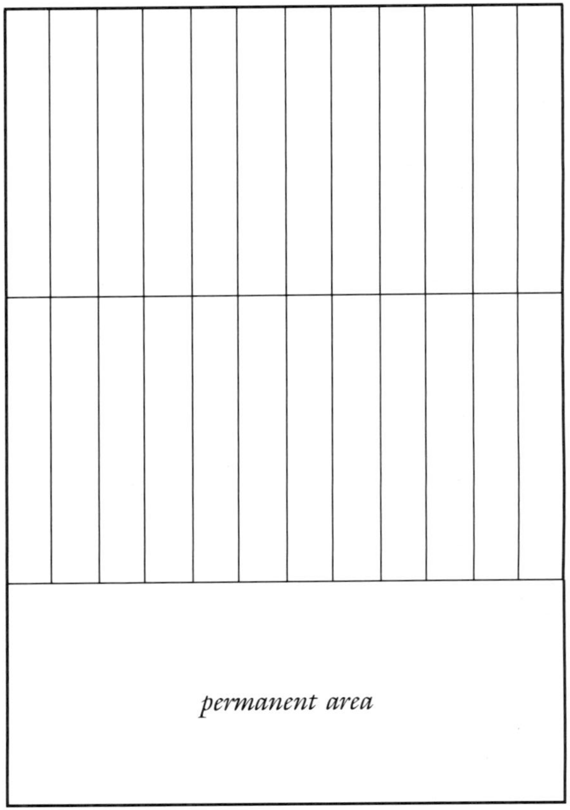

permanent area

Figure 10a: Rows across the width of your allotment or garden
24 rows each 4.5 m long, 80 cm apart (15 ft × 32 in)

permanent crops, compost, sheds, etc.

the same length, so you only need to measure one of them, but if your garden is an irregular shape you will need to measure each row and make a record of it. The problems raised by irregularly-shaped gardens are considered in some detail in Chapter 10.

You are now in a position to return to the drawing board and start planning. But I think before we go any further we should consider just what we mean here by 'a row'. Obviously its normal meaning is the line along which we plant our crops. But when we speak of 'hoeing a row of lettuces' we are obviously referring to a wider area than this. In fact, what is usually meant is to hoe some way either side of the lettuces, probably as far as half-way to the next row or even further. Similarly, when we speak of 'manuring a row' we are not suggesting that we just spread manure along the line. It should be spread over an area where the roots are, which is again a band extending some distance either side of the plants. I would suggest that you spread manure roughly 14cm (5½ inches) each side of the line making a band of 28cm width (11 inches), the centre of which is marked on your plans as 'the row'. I am going to call this band of manured soil 'the fertile band'.

The usual width of a spade is roughly 20cm (8 inches) so this means that when you are trenching you will dig a trench 20cm wide and then slide down 4cm each side to straighten up the edge. The reason for mentioning this at this point is that it means that for many vegetables (e.g. leeks, broad beans, carrots, etc.) it is possible to get a double or even, in some cases, treble row within the fertile band. This is important when you come to decide on how much space or how many rows to devote to each vegetable. This will be discussed in more detail in Chapter 5.

You now have a list of the main vegetables you want to grow and a list of the number of rows and inter-rows and their lengths. It is now a question of matching the two. In this chapter I do not propose to set out examples of plans for different needs and preferences, but rather to explore, step by step, the *process* of planning so that you can work out a plan to suit yourself. To do this, I shall take a fairly simple example and work out a plan for it. Then we shall consider some of the difficulties that can arise when things are not so simple. I shall continue with our piece of land measuring 30 feet (9.15m) by 45 feet (13.225m), with its twenty-four half rows each 4.5m long, with 80cm between each row. The crops I have selected are based on the 'Family-sized seed collection' offered by Dobies, the seed merchants. This would not be quite my personal selection; nevertheless, it obviously contains a range of crops that has been selected by popular demand, and therefore I feel it represents a useful yardstick by which to judge the method. But because it is a little bit conventional I have added a few extra vegetables, some of which come under the category 'unusual' to bring the total up to thirty-six. In Table 2 there is a list of the crops:

In Table 2, those crops marked with an asterisk (*) are sown or planted out in the summer and stand over into the winter, or are those summer crops that are too large to intercrop between them. These are the crops which have to grow in your main rows (in the fertile band) and which form the basis of your plan. There are also two crops that are not planted until the autumn (spring cabbage and broad beans) that also stand over the winter. The crops marked with a D are those winter crops which should be grown in double or treble rows, each row normally coming

Table 2: Dobies' selection of crops

Pea Kelvedon Wonder	First early	Sow March/April	Crops in 12 weeks
*Pea Onward	Main crop	Sow March/April	Crops in 15 weeks
*Broad bean Dreadnought		Sow February/April	Crops in 16 weeks
Dwarf bean Masterpiece		Sow May/June	Crops in 12 weeks
*Runner bean Scarlet Emperor		Sow May/June	Crops August onwards
*Beet Detroit	D	Sow April for summer crop, June/July for winter crop	
*Borecole		Plant out early August for winter crop	
*Broccoli, Early Purple Sprouting		Plant out June/July for cropping next March/April	
*Brussels Sprouts Roodnerf		Plant out June for winter crop	
Cabbage Golden Acre	Summer cabbage	Sow April/May	Crops in 12–14 weeks
*Cabbage Savoy Best of All		Plant out June/July for winter cropping	
Carrot Feonia	Summer crop		
*Carrot Autumn King	Winter crop D	Sow late June/July	
Cauliflower All the Year Round	Summer crop	Sow March/May	Crops 4–5 months after sowing
Cucumber Burpee		Sow or plant out late May	
*Leek Musselburgh	D	Plant out May/June for winter crop	
Lettuce All the Year Round		Sow from spring onwards for summer crops	
Lettuce Paris White (cos)		Sow from spring onwards for summer crops	
Onion Bedford Champion		Sow spring for August crop	
Spring onion White Lisbon		Sow spring onwards	
*Parsnip Intermediate	Can be D	Sow March/April for winter crop	
Radish Cherry Belle		Successional sowing throughout summer	
*Swede Acme	Can be D	Sow June for winter crop	
*Tomato Harbinger		Plant out early June	
*Turnip Model White	D	Spring onwards for summer crop, end of July for winter crop	
*Vegetable Marrow Green Bush		Sow or plant out June	
Additional vegetables			
*Sweet corn		Sow or plant out June	
*Salsify	Can be D	Sow April for winter crop	
Endive		Spring/summer for summer/autumn crop	
Chicory Rosso	D	Spring/summer for summer/winter crop	
Land cress	D	Sow summer for winter crop	
Finocchio	D	Sow July/August for September/November crop	
*Jerusalem artichoke		Plant March/April for winter crop	
*Broad bean (Aquadulce)	D	Sow November for crop in June/July following year	
*Kohlrabi	D	Sow spring/summer - crops in 12 weeks	
*Spring cabbage	Can be D	Plant out September/October for crop following spring/early summer.	

Key:
* Crops that are sown or planted out in summer and stand over into winter, or summer crops too large to intercrop between
D Winter crops that should be grown in double or treble rows within the fertile band

within the fertile band. This will need to be borne in mind when deciding upon the allocation of space. There are nineteen asterisked crops (apart from broad beans and spring cabbage) and, if you remember, we have twelve full rows or twenty-four half rows, so you will see that five crops can occupy a full row and fourteen will occupy a half row. Of course, you do not have to think in terms of rows and half rows; you can divide a half row into two, or you can divide a full row into thirds and so on. You may not, for example, want a double row of parsnips 4.5m long, which could give you 100 medium-sized parsnips or over 40 large ones. And, as you will see, I have allocated one and a half rows to brussels sprouts – partly because sprouts are one of the major winter standbys and partly because the Dobies selection had no late-winter cabbage or cauliflower. I have also given only half a row each to turnips and kohlrabi.

The next task is to allocate these main crops (those marked with an asterisk) to the rows in your garden. I have allocated them rather arbitrarily except that I have placed all the brassica family (cabbages, sprouts, turnips, etc.) at one end and the other crops at the other. But you may have to take into account your site, whether you still have crops growing from last year, whether row 12 is suitable for tomatoes, and so on.

You will find there is an advantage in putting this information on a plan of your garden because this makes it much easier to judge how things are shaping and see at a glance where there is space for your summer crops. However, I am now going to anticipate Chapter 10 and show how this plan can be made more useful still. Figure 11 shows a plan of your garden and its rows, and lists the main crops you will be growing and when to plant them. If you look back to Figure 9 you will see that there we listed (for two rows only) not only what you are going to grow (summer crops, winter crops, etc.) but when they are to be sown, harvested, etc., so that if you want to know the state of your garden

Figure 11: Plan of main crops to be sown

1a	Jerusalem artichokes (plant March)	Marrow Followed by	1b
2a	Summer broad beans (Feb/Mar to July/Aug)	Courgette Broad bean Sweet corn sown Cucumber Oct/Nov	2b
3a	Runner beans (May–Sept)	Maincrop peas (March–Sept)	3b
4a	Leeks (plant out June)	Leeks	4b
5a	Maincrop carrot (sow June/July)	Maincrop beetroot (sown June/July)	5b
6a	Parsnip (sow April)	Salsify (sow April)	6b
7a	Kale (sow June/July)	Sprouts (plant June)	7b
8a	Sprouts (plant out June)	Sprouts (plant June)	8b
9a	Purple sprouting broccoli (plant June)	Purple sprouting broccoli (plant June)	9b
10a	Cabbage (plant July)	Cabbage (plant July)	10b
11a	Swede (sow June)	Turnip/kohlrabi (sow July/August)	11b
12a	Tomatoes (plant June – Aug/Sept) followed by spring cabbage	Tomatoes followed by spring cabbage	12b

at any time all you have to do is to look downwards under the appropriate date. For example, under 'mid-summer' you can see that you will have finished harvesting very early summer vegetables in row 1, and will be planting or sowing winter vegetables. In row 2 you will have harvested over-wintered crops and will also be planting out winter vegetables. In the space between you will have a summer crop coming to maturity and perhaps just starting to be harvested. You cannot read this off easily from Figure 11 on page 43.

The next stage then is to reorganise this information as shown in Figure 12. This is all explained in greater detail in Chapter 10 because it is essential to understand it fully when it comes to crop rotation. Here we are using the plan on a rather simpler level. In Figure 12 I have not written 'sow' or 'transplant', etc. To save space, clarify and simplify the diagram I have indicated this with a line, the downwards bar indicating the approximate date of planting or sowing. Similarly, I have indicated the finish of the crop with a similar bar when the crop is lifted all at one time (such as purple sprouting broccoli) and with a dotted line when it is harvested over a period (such as leeks). The latter means that if you start harvesting the crop from one end and work down the row, some of the row will be ready for a new crop much earlier than the date when the crop is finally harvested. You will see that this second diagram enables you to read off information much more readily than the first. To give an example, if you wanted to intercrop some large Webbs Wonderful lettuces to be harvested up to the end of June, glance down the June/July columns and you will see that rows 5a and 5b are both possibilities, as are rows 10a and 10b. Such a diagram makes the planning of your summer

vegetables much easier.

Remember that this diagram is not a plan of your garden, with the lines across representing rows of crops; it simply tells you what is going on at any one time or over a period. To give one more example, if you want to know the state of play at the beginning of June, you look down the page under 'June' and see that it is as follows (this does not, of course, take into account the summer crops which we have not yet worked out):

Row 1a   Artichokes growing fast.
Rows 1b and 2b   Marrows, cucumber and sweet corn just planted or just about to be.
Row 2a   Double row of broad beans growing and probably in flower.
Row 3a   Runner beans just sown or planted (perhaps half or two-thirds of this row has been left for later sowing).
Row 3b   Maincrop peas growing (again, possibly some of the row is still empty waiting for a later sowing).
Row 4a   Double row of leeks just planted.
Row 4b   Same as 4a.
Rows 5a and 5b   Empty.
Row 6a   Double row of parsnips growing.
Row 6b   Double row of salsify growing.
Row 7a   Empty.
Rows 7b and 8b   As row 8a.
Row 8a   Sprouts just planted out or just about to be.
Row 9a   Empty (broccoli soon to be planted).
Row 9b   As row 9a.
Rows 10a and 10b   Empty.
Row 11a   Swede just sown or just about to be.
Row 11b   Empty.

Row 12a Tomatoes just planted.
Row 12b As row 12a.

By using this information and the diagram you can now see where to fit in your summer crops either in the main rows if the summer crop can be lifted before the main crops are due to be sown or planted, or between the main rows. Obviously some crops are much easier to fit in than others and I do not think you will have many problems with growing enough lettuces, summer carrots, beetroot, turnips, radishes, spring onions, land cress or endive. But before looking at these it is best to consider how to fit in the summer crops that are likely to present problems.

Cauliflower, cabbage
Although we are not yet concerned with rotations I do have a disinclination to grow brassicas (or potatoes) year after year in the same area. That is why I have gathered all the brassicas together at one end of the garden so that I can simply grow them at the other end the following year. For the same reason, I prefer to grow my summer brassicas (cabbage, cauliflower, turnip, kohlrabi, radish) in the same area; that is, from rows 7 to 12. Summer cabbage takes about twelve weeks to come to maturity. It can be sown in boxes or small pots (which will be dealt with in Chapter 5) and planted out in April for harvesting in June, or sown *in situ* in April/May for harvesting in July/August. Cauliflowers take rather longer, and you are not likely to get a crop before the end of July (and, of course, whereas a cabbage can be picked for greens before it is fully mature, an immature cauliflower is not a cauliflower at all). Cauliflowers, too, are very greedy plants, and it is an advantage to grow them in the fertile band. Both row 10b preceding late-planted winter cab-

bage or 11b preceding winter turnips are possible, and if you want slightly later ones, consider the following: plant out sprouts in late June, sprouting broccoli in July and kale in late July. These will be planted about 75cm apart (30 inches) – the kale nearer 60cm (24 inches); the plants at this stage will be quite small and they will not have reached any great size within six weeks. This would enable you to plant summer cauliflowers in the fertile band between the sprouts or broccoli. If you want them later than this – and as Dobies have not included any winter cauliflowers in their list I would certainly want to grow some autumn cauliflowers – then the cauliflowers would have to oust some other winter crop. My own preference would be to relegate the swedes to an inter-row, for example, between winter turnips and spring greens (row 11b/12b). This would mean that in their early stages they will be uncomfortably close to your tomatoes in row 12b. This will not harm them but it will make it difficult to get at the tomatoes. However, they can on this occasion be easily reached from the other side. Possibly also, if you have a greenhouse you will not want to grow a whole 30 foot (9.15cm) row of outdoor tomatoes, in which case your autumn cauliflowers could grow there and be followed by late planted spring cabbage. Summer cabbages do not present such a problem as they will be out of the ground earlier. In fact, you can probably sow a complete row and harvest first the ones that are situated where your sprouts will grow. If you want late summer and autumn cabbages I would prefer to grow here a smaller variety such as minicole. I think I would also prefer the cauliflower Snowball to All the Year Round as, again, it is slightly smaller. Minicole is too slow-growing for the early summer cabbages so you

Figure 12: Diagram showing main crops and sowing and harvesting times over one season

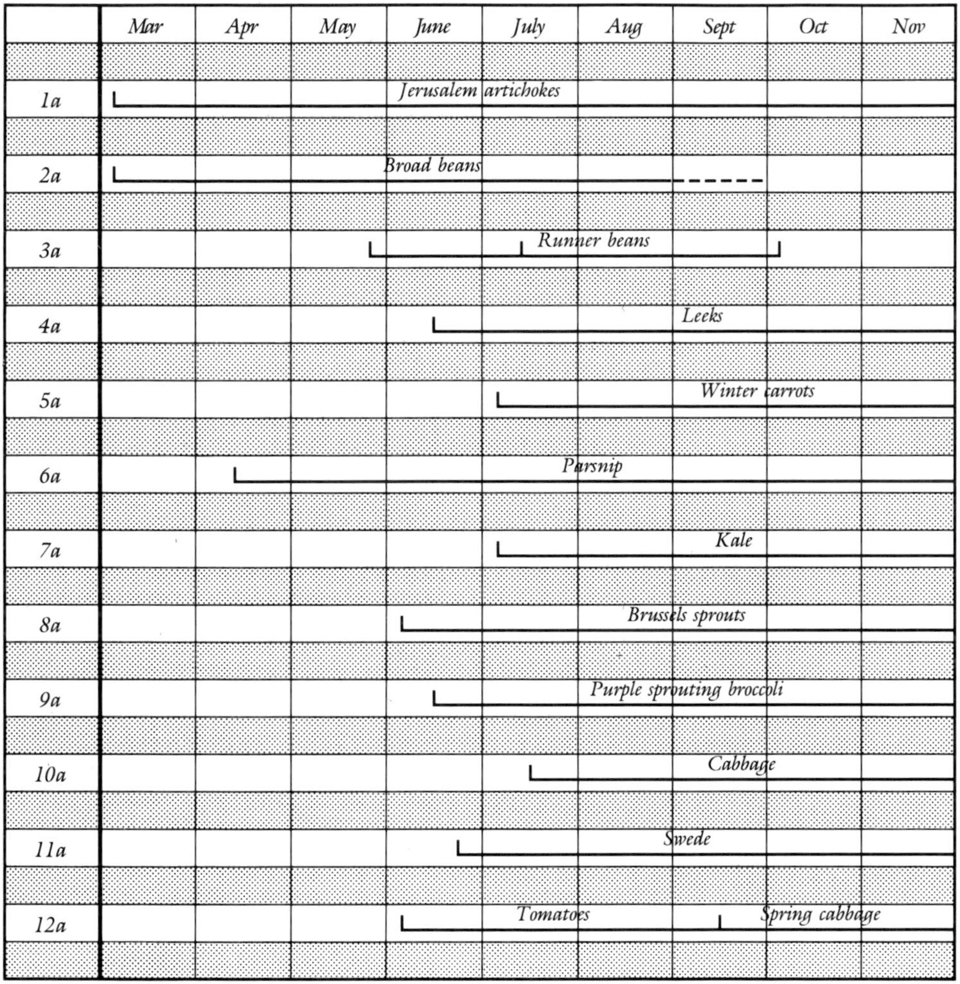

	Mar	Apr	May	June	July	Aug	Sept	Oct	Nov
1a				Jerusalem artichokes					
2a				Broad beans					
3a					Runner beans				
4a				Leeks					
5a					Winter carrots				
6a				Parsnip					
7a				Kale					
8a				Brussels sprouts					
9a				Purple sprouting broccoli					
10a				Cabbage					
11a				Swede					
12a				Tomatoes		Spring cabbage			

Key:

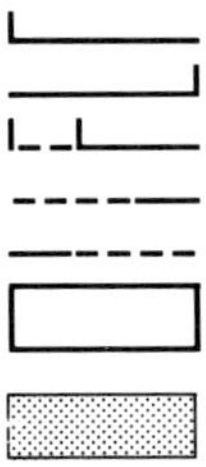

└────── the crop is all sown or planted at the same time
──────┘ the crop is all lifted at the same time
└─ ─└────── the soil is best undisturbed from the first marker until the crop is planted at the second
─ ─ ─ ─ ─ the crop is sown over a period
─ ─ ─ ─ ─ the crop is lifted over a period

[   ] crops grown across the rows

 intercropping rows

Mar	Apr	May	June	July	Aug	Sept	Oct	Nov	
									1b
			Marrow					Broad	
			Courgette					Beans	
			Sweet corn						2b
			Cucumber						
									3b
		Maincrop peas							
									4b
			Leeks						
									5b
			Beetroot						
									6b
		Salsify							
									7b
			Brussels sprouts						
									8b
			Brussels sprouts						
									9b
			Purple sprouting broccoli						
									10b
			Cabbage						
									11b
			Turnip/kohlrabi						
									12b
		Tomatoes			Spring cabbage				

Note: Times for sowing, harvesting and so on are based on when these events would take place in the south of England. Variations due to weather and other factors specific to your area will need to be taken into account.

would need a variety such as Golden Acre as well.

It is a good idea to mark out with short sticks the exact positions where your sprouts, etc., will go so that if the planting of cabbages or cauliflowers or other summer crops precedes that of the sprouts you will know exactly where to plant them. Figure 13 shows the positioning for these crops.

Early peas
Peas sown in March will be harvested in June. Peas sown in April will be harvested in July. Peas sown in May will be harvested in August.

March and April sown peas could, therefore, go in any of the main rows not being used at those times; e.g., in rows 5 or 10. May sown peas present a problem as the garden will be getting pretty crowded in August when they are ready for harvesting. However, by this time your first batch of maincrop

peas should be in full swing, so I think May-sown Kelvedon Wonder is a crop you will have to forego.

Dwarf bean
These take up quite a bit of space and would be difficult to intercrop. One possibility is to take some of the row allocated to broad beans or runner beans. All beans are very prolific and there is always a danger of being overwhelmed with them during August and September. On the other hand, beans are very useful for freezing, so another possibility is to reduce both parsnip and salsify to a 10 foot (3m) row and grow dwarf beans in the 10 foot (3m) between them. There would be room for a double row in the fertile band, giving you thirty plants.

Finocchio
You will notice that in the diagram I

Figure 13: Rows 7a, 8a and 9a in June showing positions where main crops (X) will be planted and where intercrops are growing

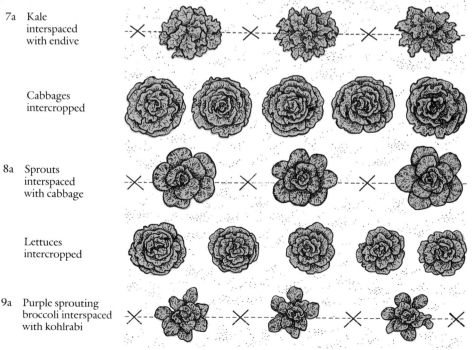

7a Kale interspaced with endive

Cabbages intercropped

8a Sprouts interspaced with cabbage

Lettuces intercropped

9a Purple sprouting broccoli interspaced with kohlrabi

have given two dates for sowing and harvesting runner beans and peas. This is because you have a full 4.5m (15 feet) for each of these which is a generous allowance. You will not want all these coming into harvest at once. If you make an early sowing of half the row of peas and aim to lift it in late July when your second sowing in April is just coming into bearing you can follow the early crops with finocchio. It is possible to transplant finocchio if you are careful, so thinnings from this sowing could be planted out in mid-August to follow the first half-row of runner beans.

Onions

Onions are a bit of a problem as they need to be sown or planted in early spring and will not be ready for lifting before August. Onions can be sown in rows 15cm (6 inches) apart, the individual plants 10–20cm apart in the rows, depending on whether you prefer large or small onions (the total crop will be about the same by weight). You can, therefore, intercrop a double row between broccoli and cabbage (9b/10b) and another row between cabbage and turnip (10b/11b). This would give you about ninety large onions or 240 smaller ones. This, by the way, would not be within your fertile band so quite an amount of compost would have to be worked into the top four inches of the soil. If you are a keen onion grower then you may prefer to look carefully at your fertile bands and decide which crops have to be sacrificed.

Kohlrabi

This is a crop somewhat similar to turnip, occupying much the same space but taking up to twelve weeks to grow – but do not let it get too large because, like turnips, it is inclined to become woody if allowed to grow beyond cricket-ball size. It has the advantage that it can be transplanted. As a summer crop it could be treated like cabbage and planted between sprouts and/or purple sprouting broccoli, or it can precede winter turnips or cabbage.

This about finishes the 'difficult' summer crops. I need hardly say that working out this plan should be done with a pencil – with an eraser close to hand. You will have to shuffle crops around a bit and, depending on your choice, you may have to accept that you cannot grow quite everything you had hoped. Once you have fixed the position of these 'difficult' crops you can turn to the easy ones and fit them wherever there is a space.

Lettuce

Unless you buy plants or raise them yourself under cover, you will find that outdoor spring-sown lettuce will come to maturity in June. It is possible to obtain 'leaf lettuce' quite quickly within six or seven weeks from sowing, by sowing in rows 4½ inches (12cm) apart and thinning the plants to 1 inch (2.5cm). You can pick the young leaves and leave the stumps to produce a second and third crop. If you sow successional crops you can have leaf lettuce from mid-May onwards until your hearted lettuces are ready for cutting. Paris White, Lobjots or Little Gem are all suitable varieties for this.

Endive

Since these require attention (blanching by bunching up the leaves and tying them together) it is a good idea to plant them where they can be easily reached – say as an edging to a path. Endive can also be grown where winter cabbages or other brassicas are to follow because when the leaves are bunched up tightly for blanching each plant only takes up about 8 inches (12cm) of space: then every other one is picked early and this will leave plenty of room for planting out cabbages in the space. Endive should be sown from March onwards and take 14–16 weeks to mature. It is not a completely hardy crop but will probably survive without protection until Christmas or until the first hard frost.

Chicory Rosso
This is principally a winter crop. During the summer it sends up large green leaves rather like an open cos lettuce. You can pick these in moderation but they are rather bitter (not so bitter as the similar looking Witloof Chicory, though). In the winter the green leaves die down and the plant develops an attractive dark red rosette. Like endive, it makes an attractive edging. It is completely hardy and will go to seed in April.

Land cress
This is also a winter salad crop, sown in late summer. It takes up very little space and can be grown as an edging plant or under tall crops, especially those whose foliage dies down in the winter such as parsnip or salsify or, as I have placed it here, artichokes. It is very hardy.

Summer carrots, beetroot, turnips, radish and spring onion
These are all fairly small plants which can be grown successively between major crops.

We shall now fill in the summer crops in our plan. This is shown in Figure 14. This is not, of course, the only possible plan, and I make no claim that it is the best one because everything depends on the vegetables and the quantities of them you want to grow. I give it merely as an example of how to fit crops in to make full use of your space. I will now run down the rows and make a few brief comments:

Rows 1a/2a   Jerusalem artichokes take up quite a lot of space and make a lot of shade. Broad beans will be in a double row but can be picked from the other side. So there is room for a double row of leaf lettuce which can be lifted in July as soon as your full lettuces come to maturity, to be replaced by a double row of land cress to stand the winter.

Rows 2a/3a and 3a/4a   No room for intercropping as runner beans will need all the space you can spare. Have at least two sowings, a month or six weeks apart. Lift the early one mid-August, even if there are still beans on it, as there will be plenty to come from later sowings, and replace with a double row of finocchio.

Row 4a   You may be able to plant leeks out later than June (see Chapter 5) which would provide an opportunity to grow an early crop here.

Row 5a   Precede carrots with early peas, again leaving no space for intercropping. Sow the carrots in a triple or quadruple row, using space between 5a and 4a and between 5a and 6a.

Row 6a   One third of this row goes to a double row of dwarf beans. They need quite a bit of attention usually, so do not intercrop here. The parsnips will be grown in a double row and you could intercrop further rows if you like parsnips.

Rows 6a/7a   Intercrop with autumn cabbages. As mentioned above it is better to grow the smallest variety you can get hold of; for example, minicole.

Row 7a   Grow a full row of endive and lift early the ones growing where the kale is to be planted. Measure out these stations and mark them with sticks so that you remember.

Row 8a   Kohlrabi grown between the stations for the sprouts. If you start these in March you could sow a whole row and then lift early the ones where the sprouts are to be planted.

Row 9a   Kohlrabi (as 8a) or turnip.

Row 10a   Early peas to precede cabbage, leaving no room for intercropping.

Row 11a   You can grow a summer crop here to be lifted in late June. If you sow swedes later than early June you will get smaller swedes, so thin them closer together (6 inches (15cm) instead of 9 inches (23cm)). But, as I have already explained, you may prefer to grow autumn cauliflower here.

Row 12a   You can plant two or three rows of spring cabbage close together, lifting every other one, or two out of three, for spring greens and letting the remainder grow on to heart in the late spring or early summer.

Plant alternative endive and chicory for an edging. The endive will only survive mild frosts but the chicory should survive the winter.

Row 1b/2b   Spread sweet corn, courgette, etc , over two rows. In late autumn follow with two double rows of over-wintering broad beans.

Row 3b   Maincrop peas. Have at least two sowings, following the first by finocchio. There is no room for intercropping.

Row 4b   Leeks, as 4a.

Row 4b/5b   Summer carrots. Several rows. Sow and use the ones in the fertile row first, to make way for the beetroot.

Row 6b   Allow a third of the row for dwarf beans, as in row 6a.

Row 7b   As 7a, or grow early summer cabbage to interspace between the sprouts.

Row 7b/8b   There is room for two or three rows of radish here.

Row 8b   There is room here for a row of summer cauliflower, interspaced with the sprouts, but only if they are planted out early in April.

Row 8b/9b   Spring onions; room for several rows grown in succession.

Row 9b   Summer cauliflower precedes and overlaps the broccoli.

Row 9b/10b/11b   Intercrop double row onions each side. Lift them as soon as they have wilted and dry them off elsewhere to make room for cabbages, which can be grown in a triple row as in 10a.

Row 11b   Precede winter turnips and kohlrabi with summer turnips. The kohlrabi can be transplanted as late as mid-August.

Row 12b   As 12a.

When we started this plan we made our task easier by assuming we had a completely unoccupied piece of land, but of course this is not usually the case. Usually you will have a number of crops over-wintered from the previous year still occupying land until April, May or June. So, let us continue with this plan and see how it leaves us in the following year. There will still be crops in the following rows.

Row 1a   Artichokes will start sprouting as soon as the warmer weather comes, but you can go on lifting them till May.

Row 1a/2a   Land cress can be left until it goes to seed.

Rows 1b and 2b   It is a good idea to pinch out one row of broad beans when it has three flower trusses, to produce an early crop which will be harvested in early June. Pick it hard and lift it before the end of June even if there are still some pods unpicked, as you will need the space. The second row can follow to fill in until the spring-sown crop is ready. Leave a few plants at the end of the row to

Figure 14: Summer and winter vegetables for one season (summmer vegetables in green)

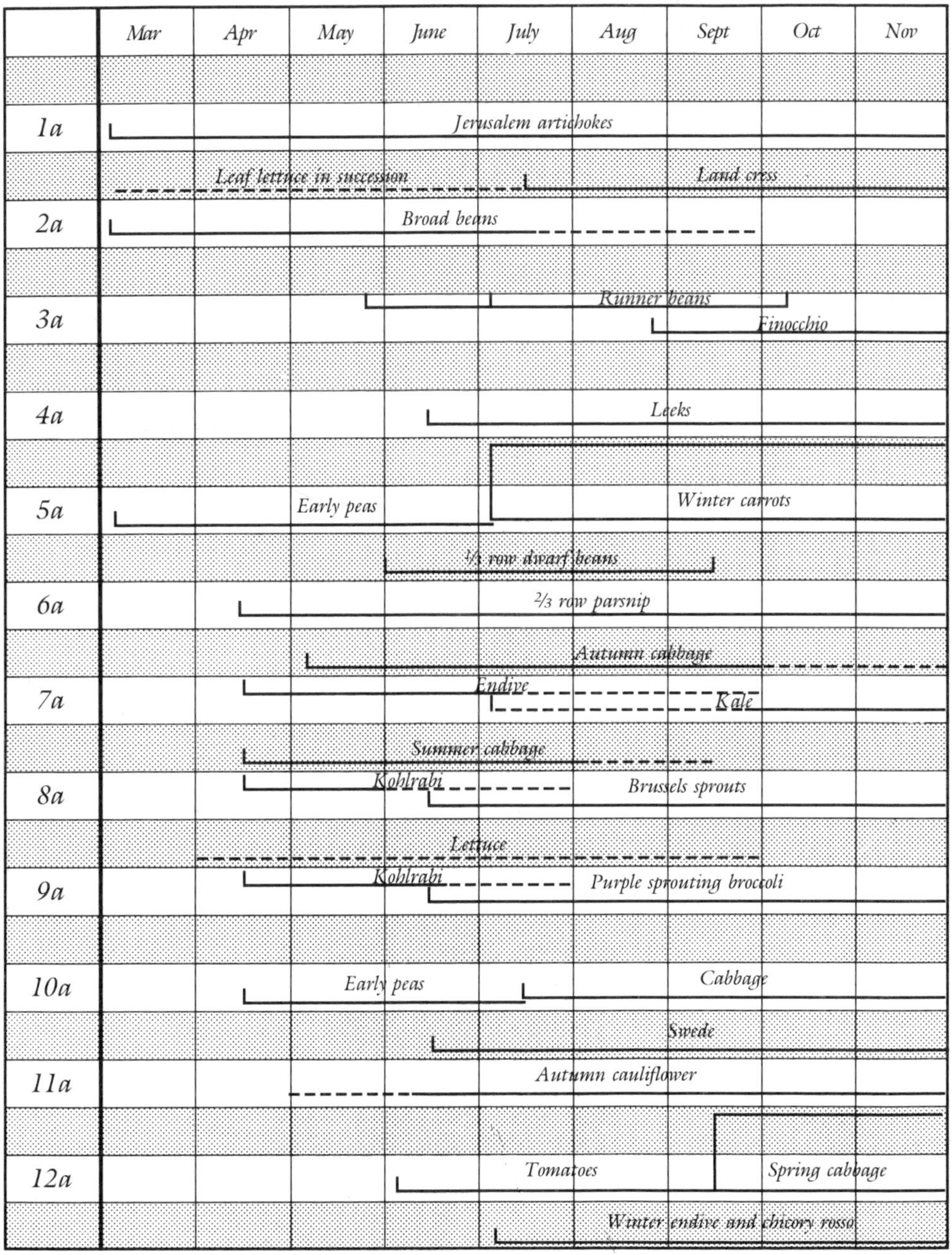

	Mar	Apr	May	June	July	Aug	Sept	Oct	Nov
1a				Jerusalem artichokes					
2a		Leaf lettuce in succession					Land cress		
				Broad beans					
3a					Runner beans			Finocchio	
4a						Leeks			
5a			Early peas				Winter carrots		
6a				⅓ row dwarf beans					
					⅔ row parsnip				
7a					Endive	Autumn cabbage	Kale		
8a			Summer cabbage				Brussels sprouts		
			Kohlrabi						
9a			Lettuce				Purple sprouting broccoli		
			Kohlrabi						
10a			Early peas				Cabbage		
11a				Swede					
				Autumn cauliflower					
12a				Tomatoes			Spring cabbage		
						Winter endive and chicory rosso			

Mar	Apr	May	June	July	Aug	Sept	Oct	Nov	
									1b
				Marrow				Broad	
				Courgette				Beans	
				Sweet corn					
				Cucumber					2b
				Maincrop peas			Finocchio		3b
					Leeks				4b
			Carrots						
		Carrots							5b
				Beetroot					
		Carrots		⅓ row dwarf beans					
				⅔ row salsify					6b
			Lettuce						
		Summer cabbage			Brussels sprouts				7b
		Radish							
	Summer cauliflower				Brussels sprouts				8b
		Spring onion							
		Summer cauliflower				Purple sprouting broccoli			9b
		Onions							
		Onions				Cabbage			10b
		Onions							
		Summer turnips			Turnip/kohlrabi				11b
				Tomatoes		Spring cabbage			12b
				Winter endive and chicory rosso					

produce the next year's seed.

Row 4a or 4b   Most of the leeks will have been lifted but some will remain until they begin to go to seed in late April or May. We can choose whether to leave these late ones in row 4a or 4b depending upon the crops we wish to follow them.

Row 6a   Parsnips can be left in the ground until they begin to sprout. This depends a bit on the weather.

Row 6b   The same applies to salsify. Their green shoots are edible either blanched or green, though no dish for a gourmet.

Row 7a   Kale. This will go to seed in April/May and you will probably continue to crop it up to these months.

Rows 7b, 8a and 8b   Brussels sprouts. These will go on producing greens even after the actual sprouts are finished. You may wish to leave a few for this up to the end of April.

Row 9a/9b   Purple sprouting broccoli. The Dobies list specified 'early' which will be out of the ground by the end of March. But if we had preferred the late variety (as, in fact, I personally would have done) it would have stayed cropping till early May.

Row 11a   Swedes can remain in the ground until they start sprouting, and perhaps these early months when vegetables are scarce is when they come into their own.

Row 12a/12b   Spring cabbage will be harvested through April and May as spring greens, and up to July as headed cabbage. We can choose whether to leave the latest ones in row 12a or 12b.

Row 12a/12b   Chicory will continue to produce salading until it runs to seed.

This situation is shown in Figure 15.

I have said we are not concerned with a strict rotation in this early part of the book, but I do recommend that as far as possible you should avoid growing the same crops in the same rows in successive years – particularly brassicas, potatoes and onions. Since Dobies did not include potatoes (and nor did I) this means that in the second year we grow brassicas and onions in rows 1 to 6 and all the other main crops in rows 7 to 12 and we will now check the possibility of this. I am assuming, by the way, that we are growing exactly the same crops as last year, though in practice this would probably not be the case as most people do like to try out new varieties and new crops each year.

In Figure 16 I have filled in the succession to follow the previous year's crops. As you will see, this does not present any great difficulty and does not limit the crops you want to grow. When it comes to fitting in the summer crops there will be some problems and, indeed, some limitations because of the overwintered crops still growing. But I think that by now you will know that you can shift crops around on your plan to fit your summer vegetables in to best advantage. I will leave you to work this one out for yourself.

The above plans are, of course, not the only possible ones; they are given merely as examples of how to fit crops in and to use your space. To finish this chapter I will list the crops I would grow if I had to limit myself to thirty-six and had half an allotment to grow them in. I have not included crops such as asparagus, globe artichoke and seakale etc., which would be grown in permanent positions. I have tried to ensure that some crops are coming to maturity every month of the year (April, May and June present the most problems, of course) and that there is a good mixture between salad crops, conventional crops and experimental and/or unusual ones. The crops I would choose are:

Jerusalem artichoke

Broad bean   autumn sown for following June/July

French bean   Blue Lake — a prolific climber of high quality which would share one row with runners

Runner bean   one of the modern stringless varieties

Beetroot   Detroit New Globe or similar variety suitable for summer and winter

Sprouting broccoli   late variety

Brussels sprouts   Roodnerf has a long season

Cabbage winter probably January King

Savoy   Ormskirk Late Spring

Carrots   Amsterdam forcing for earlier Chantenay red-cored for maincrop

Cauliflower winter   I would choose two varieties for April and May

Celeriac

Chicory   Witloof for chicons Rosso, or one of the other varieties stocked by the HDRA

Cress   American land cress

Cucumber   one of the new hybrids

Endive   there is a wide variety which I would ring changes on over the years

Finocchio

Kohlrabi   the purple variety because it looks more decorative

Figure 15: Overwintered crops in season succeeding Figure 14

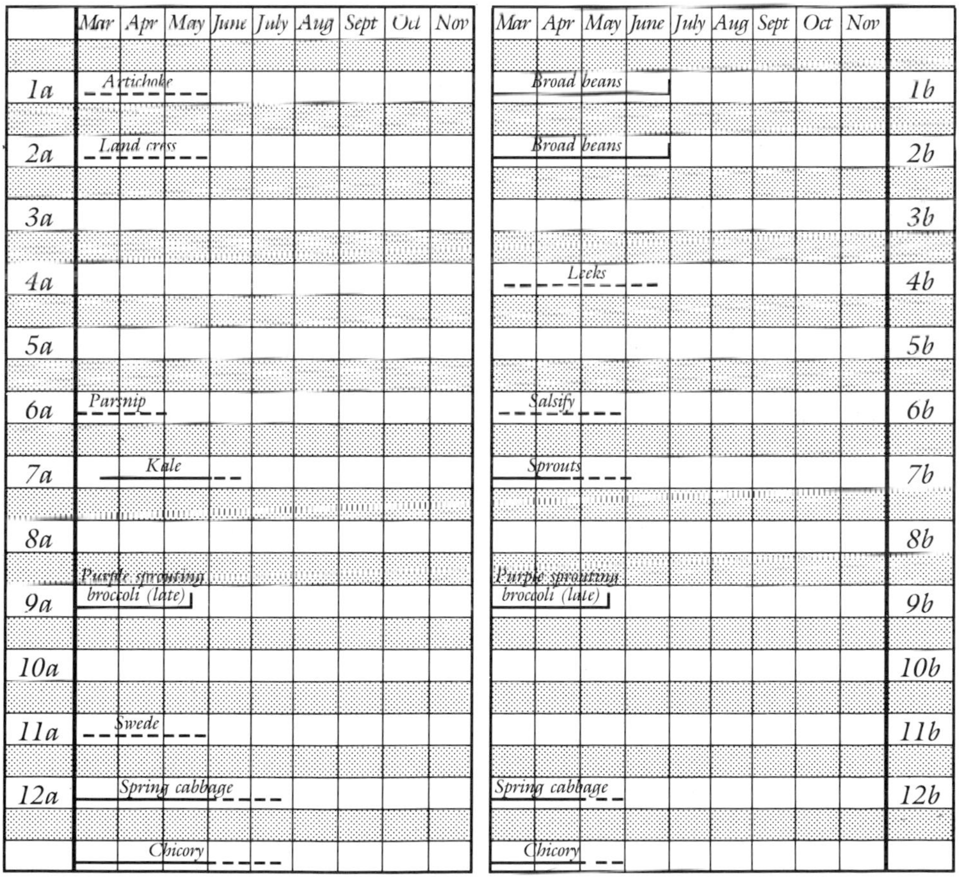

	Mar	Apr	May	June	July	Aug	Sept	Oct	Nov	
1a		Artichoke								1b — Broad beans
2a		Land cress								2b — Broad beans
3a										3b
4a										4b — Leeks
5a										5b
6a		Parsnip								6b — Salsify
7a			Kale							7b — Sprouts
8a										8b
9a		Purple sprouting broccoli (late)								9b — Purple sprouting broccoli (late)
10a										10b
11a		Swede								11b
12a		Spring cabbage								12b — Spring cabbage
			Chicory							Chicory

	Mar	Apr	May	June	July	Aug	Sept	Oct	Nov
1a	Artichoke	Early peas					Cabbage		
2a	Land cress					Purple sprouting broccoli			
3a		Onions					Kale		
4a		Onions				Brussels sprouts			
5a				Tomatoes followed by spring cabbage					
6a	Parsnip				Swede				
7a	Kale			Runner beans					
8a					Parsnips				
9a	Purple sprouting broccoli (late)			Leeks					
10a				Artichokes					
11a	Swede			Summer broad beans					
12a	Spring cabbage			Winter carrots					
	Chicory								

Mar	Apr	May	June	July	Aug	Sept	Oct	Nov	
		Broad beans				Cabbage			1b
		Broad beans			Purple sprouting broccoli				2b
				Brussels sprouts					3b
	Leeks			Brussels sprouts					4b
				Tomatoes followed by spring cabbage					5b
	Salsify				Winter turnip				6b
Brussels sprouts				Salsify					7b
				Peas					8b
Purple sprouting broccoli (late)				Leeks					9b
	Early peas				Beetroot				10b
			Marrow / Cucumber / Sweet corn				Broad Beans		11b
Spring cabbage									12b
Chicory									

Lettuce   ring changes on various lettuces over the years

Courgettes   most courgettes can be grown on to produce small marrows

Onions   Japanese – autumn sown sets

Parsnip

Peas   maincrop I might go for petit pois even though it is not a prolific producer
early Kelvedon Wonder takes a lot of beating

Potato   early

Radish   winter – Chinese or Black Spanish

Salsify ⎫
Scorzonera ⎭   I would ring the changes between these two

Spinach beet ⎫
Seakale beet ⎭   and these two

Sweet corn   I would try to find a hybrid that produces several cobs per plant instead of just one or two

Tomato   I find Harbinger hard to beat

Turnip

I would also grow garlic, parsley and sorrel, but have only managed to stay within the prescribed thirty-six crops by relegating these to the herb garden. To be frank I am not entirely happy with this selection because it omits crops I hate to be without, such as Chinese cabbage, calabrese, many more peas, etc., but in this list I am thinking in terms of one year. In reality there are many years stretching ahead, the seasons succeed each other and each year you can try out new varieties and crops.

CHAPTER 5
IMPROVING PERFORMANCE

The usual cursory advice given in gardening books is 'These operations should be carried out two or three weeks later in the North of England'. Certainly the planning programme I have outlined in the last chapter could easily run into trouble in an inclement spring or summer in the South of England; but in the North it would always be a risky proposition.

So how can we improve its chances of working? The main difficulty is not just that spring comes later and colder in the North, it is that the whole growing season is much shorter and more restricted, and that the colder average temperature means slower growth throughout the whole season. Consequently there is a major difficulty with congestion during this short growing season, and the problem is to ensure that early crops are harvested and out of the way before the later ones that will occupy their space are due for planting out. Obviously there are two ways of achieving this: either by advancing the early crops, or by delaying the sowing or planting out of the later ones. There are four methods which can improve one or other of these factors:

1. The use of cloches, frames, the greenhouse or the spare bedroom.
2. Sowing and growing in individual pots for transplanting.
3. The pre-germination of seeds.
4. Methods for delayed transplanting without any resulting setback in growth.

We shall consider these one by one:

1. The use of cloches, frames, the greenhouse, or the spare bedroom.
This book is not really intended to cover protected cropping, so I shall not deal with the extensive use of glass or plastic protection or with ways of making the most beneficial use of it. What I am concerned with is the temporary cover that can be given to enable spring plants to start growth some weeks earlier. Of course, most summer crops can be started off earlier with the use of cloches, but Table 3 shows a few that derive particular benefit.

I have indicated roughly the date the crop comes into harvest. I have not indicated the date harvesting is finished, and this raises an important point. You do not have to keep plants until the very last of the crops is picked. This particularly applies to crops such as peas and beans where plants will go on producing a smattering of pods long after it has ceased to be economical to keep them taking up space in the garden. Your purpose is not to pick your plant to the last pod regardless, but to use your ground in the most productive way possible and this often means lifting a crop before you have exhausted it in order to make way for the following one. So, although your cloched broad beans would go on producing a crop later than, say, mid-June it might be better to pick one of your half rows as clean as possible very young and lift

Table 3: Earliest safe sowing dates for summer crops

	Cloched	*In the open*	*Start of harvesting*
Broad beans (Longpod and Windsor)	January	March	Late May Late June
French beans	Mid April	Mid May	Early July Late July
Runner beans	Late April	June	Early July August
Cabbage	March	April	Late June Late July
Carrot	February	March	Late May Late June
Cauliflower	March	April	Mid July Late August
Lettuce (headed)	March	March/April	May June
Early potato	February	March	May June
Sweet corn	May	June	Ripening depends on the weather

them in order to make room for a following crop.

2. Sowing and growing in individual pots for transplanting.

An alternative to cloches is the kitchen window-sill, though I have often wondered why it has to be the kitchen sill which is so often already cluttered up with a whole assortment of objects; it seems to me to be the least available and least convenient window-sill. It also has the disadvantage of wide and often wild fluctuations of temperature and humidity. What is important is that the sill you use should be light and airy, that it should be relatively but steadily warm, and that there should be plenty of space, preferably to enable you to put a small table in front of it. A bedroom, preferably the spare bedroom, is more likely to meet these requirements than the kitchen. And if there is a danger of cold or even frost, it is surprising how much gentle heat a well-placed forty watt electric light bulb can provide at the equivalent cost of having a one-bar

electric fire on for one hour a day. In fact this arrangement can double up with the wine-making area for which a forty watt bulb also provides just about the right temperature.

Seed can be sown and seedlings started off in seed trays or wooden boxes, but in many cases it is worth sowing individually by using small pots. If you are thrifty it is worth collecting small yoghurt pots or plastic cups. You can stack these three or four at a time, invert them, and make three or four holes through the bottoms with a heated metal needle or 5 inch (12.5cm) nail or bradawl. You can also use 9 oz (250gm) round margarine tubs but they take up rather more space. For handling it is best to put the pots or tubs in wooden trays – the sort that you can usually pick up outside supermarkets or at vegetable markets. Choose the ones with wooden bases rather than hardboard ones as the latter rot and warp rather quickly. You should be able to fit twenty pots in each box. You need to cover everything with thick layers of newspaper to avoid creating a mess.

I do not buy potting compost because that would be too expensive for the number of plants I start this way, and also because so much of the potting compost you buy is rubbish. I once took a sample of what seemed a particularly dubious quality John Innes compost to the Trades Description people, complaining that it did not in any way match the original formula set out in the book *Seed and Potting Compost* by Lawrence and Newell. They agreed with me and sympathized, but could not take any action because the expression 'John Innes' is not a registered trade design, but merely a description of a certain kind of compost. So – beware: the description 'John Innes compost' carries no guarantee of quality or composition – which is not to say, of course, that there are not many excellent and reputable brands of it.

What I do is to empty all the residues of my potting and plant-raising activities into a bin, accumulating it throughout the year. I buy one medium-sized bag of peat and then make up the following mix: 3 parts residue, 1 part peat, 1 part finely sifted compost from the compost heap. I do not sterilize this, though I think it would be wise to do so if you have the necessary equipment – though, personally, I have only very seldom been troubled with damping off or similar problems.

I regularly start off the following crops in pots by this method often in conjunction with the pre-germination technique (see 3 below):

Tomato	Early sweet corn
Sweet pepper	Early runner and
Parsley	French bean
Onions	Marrow
Garlic	Courgette
	Cucumber

I have to admit that I do not grow a lot of onions, but nowadays confine myself mainly to autumn-sown sets to get onions in June when they are so expensive. If I did grow a lot maybe I would find this method too cumbersome and time-consuming. Similarly, for crops such as beans, I grow only a small number of plants this way, so as to get an early crop. I usually sow my main crops directly outdoors.

Many other crops could, of course, be similarly started off in this way: for example, early lettuces and endives, summer cabbage and cauliflower, and autumn-sown broad beans. With these small pots you cannot allow more than a few weeks growth and if you are really serious and want to start outdoor tomatoes and peppers early, you will have to pot them on. In this case you are into another game and had better think of buying a small greenhouse and a book on planning your greenhouse crops.

3. The pre-germination of seeds

Another way of improving your garden's performance is by pre-germinating your seeds. This method was originally developed at the National Vegetable Research Station and is described in the book *Know and Grow Vegetables*. It has since been copied or mentioned in many other books and articles. Some people have been put off by the fact that it seems quite a complicated and time-consuming process and it is true that a method that is simple and straightforward to operate when you have all the resources of a horticultural research station at your disposal may not always transfer easily to an allotment or small garden. For example, the method requires a convenient supply of water, so it certainly would not be very suitable for an allotment that is some distance from the nearest standpipe. Also it is difficult if you only garden at weekends because it is hard to judge the germination of the seed very accurately and if, through a miscalculation, the seeds do not germinate until the Monday or Tuesday after the planned weekend it is unlikely that they will keep until the following weekend. Even worse is the situation when they germinate as expected on the Saturday and it rains steadily for the whole weekend. Equally it is unwise to pre-germinate seeds in mid-summer when there is a danger of a week's dry weather or more, unless you are sure you can get out to water them. Carrot seed, for example, sown in the normal way will just remain dormant through a dry period, until the rain comes to start its germination; but pre-germinated carrot seeds, left unwatered, will wither and die. This applies to other seeds as well, of course, but carrots are particularly vulnerable as they take rather a long time to germinate. Also, although in the end it does produce better plants and saves time and trouble (because you won't have to thin them for one thing), it does take considerably longer and does involve careful planning of your time.

That said, it is remarkably successful and for some plants makes such an improvement that it is worth some trouble. Also, although for carrots and similar small-seeded crops pre-germination does necessarily involve fluid sowing, there are many cases where it does not.

I am an enthusiast for pre-germination, but normally restrict it to the following cases:

seeds that are usually planted individually anyway; e.g., beetroot, parsnip.

seeds that are not, but which are quite large enough for it to be quite easy to do so; e.g., chicory

seeds that will be sown indoors in pots or seedboxes so that you are not dependent upon the weather and can have everything you need to hand.

seeds with crops where you only have to grow a few plants so that even if sowing each seed is quite a time-consuming event, there are not many of them.

a few special cases, such as celeriac, where the problems and time spent seem well worth the result.

If you are going to take pre-germination seriously you should read a book on the subject – preferably the classic *Know and Grow Vegetables* – but bear in mind the comments I have made above. I do not feel that pre-germination is a legitimate part of planning, and so it should not occupy too much of this book. But here is an example of its value.

The average family does not eat a whole row of parsley – twelve well-grown plants should be ample. If you pre-germinate there is no need to fluid drill a row because the seed, although not large, is not difficult to handle. To pre-germinate the seed you need a small flat plastic container – a 9oz (250gm) sunflower margarine tub is suitable. Cut up or fold several layers of newspaper and lay them on the bottom, then leave them to soak in water. When they are thoroughly wet drain off the surplus water, space about twenty seeds on the paper and replace the lid. This small tub will not take up a lot of space and can be put anywhere in the house that is gently and steadily warm; for example, the airing cupboard well away from the hot tank. But it will do well enough in a corner of the living room. Examine the tub after three or four days to make sure it is not drying out (if it is you either have not wetted it enough, or you have not put enough thicknesses of paper, or you have not properly closed the lid. If it is dry you must, of course, wet it again by sprinkling water on top of it. Then after another three days you

examine it daily. The seeds should germinate about seven days from the start, but it
depends very much on the temperature.
When they do, prepare twelve pots with
your home-made (or bought) compost.
Carefully take the paper (with the seeds on
it) out of the tub and lay it on the table.
Now with a pair of tweezers or (as I find
easier) the well-wetted blunt wooden end
of a matchstick, transfer one seed (selecting ones that have obviously germinated)
into each tub and cover with a thin layer of
damp soil. If not enough seeds have germinated (and sometimes there is quite a
variation in the time they take) put the
paper back into the tub, close the lid, and
have a look next day.

The pots should be put in a box or
seedtray and covered with glass to
prevent them drying out. The seedlings
should appear in about five or six days.
Within two or three weeks they should
be showing several sturdy true leaves
and be ready for moving to somewhere
a little less protected, preparatory to
hardening off and planting out.

Quite a bit of trouble, yes. But much
better after six weeks to have nice
thriving plants just transplanted into
clean soil than be still searching
amongst the shepherds purse and the
groundsel to see whether your parsley
seeds have germinated yet.

This system can be used for all crops
for which the seed is usually individually sown (whether indoors or outdoors)
and because the seed will only be sown
when it has already germinated, there is
no need to sow more than one seed per
station (though, frankly, cautious chap
that I am, I usually sow two to be on
the safe side). It is particularly valuable
in this respect for crops such as parsnip,
salsify and scorzonera whose germination is slow and unreliable. The following crops benefit particularly from
pre-germination and none of them
require fluid drilling:

*Aubergine
*Broad bean (especially the autumn
  sown ones)
*French bean
*Runner bean
 Beetroot
 Chicory
 Courgette
 Cucumber
 Sweet fennel (finocchio)
*Parsley
*Parsnip
*Pea
*Pepper
*Potato (chitting is in effect a sort of
  pre-germination)
*Salsify
*Scorzonera
*Sweet corn
*Tomato

I have marked with an asterisk seeds
where pre-germination seems to be
particularly beneficial. Three other
crops benefit greatly from pre-
germination – carrots, leeks and lettuce,
but they involve fluid drilling. For a
description of this you should refer to
Know and Grow Vegetables (I).

Another seed that is worth pre-
germinating is celeriac. I have already
said that I do not think it is worthwhile
growing celery from seed, especially
since it is possible to buy plants and
since it is very difficult to produce celery
plants that do not bolt, unless you have
a proper thermostatically controlled
seed propagator. But you cannot usually buy celeriac plants (well, never, in my
experience) and I have found that it is
possible to raise plants from seed
without heat, and that pre-germination
makes this easier and less chancy.

Celeriac seed is as fine as dust and you
need to be very careful sprinkling it on
your wet paper to make sure the seeds
are not all bunched together. Then the
seeds must be germinated in the light

(nearly all other seeds germinate in the dark), so the top of the container must be covered with glass. It is important that there is a good thickness of wet paper and that it is thoroughly wet right through, and that the glass fits tight, as celeriac seed is very slow to germinate and you do not want it to dry out half-way through. After about ten to fourteen days it will show signs of germination (and you need a good light and good eyesight to see this) and you will probably need a magnifying glass to pick up all the seeds. You may need to sharpen your matchstick a bit (though do not sharpen it to a point). Then transfer your seeds to a pot. It is worth planting two or three seeds per pot and for this reason it may be easier on this occasion to use the wider margarine tubs than the tall yoghurt ones. Sprinkle the minimum amount of fine soil on top using a nylon kitchen sieve. As soon as you see that your seeds have taken and are showing two leaves you can reduce them to one plant per pot.

You start pre-germinating in early April, and you will not plant out until June, by which time your plants may be larger than your margarine tubs can satisfactorily accommodate, so you may have to pot them on in larger pots. All this, of course, is quite troublesome and time-consuming – but then celeriac is a unique and unequalled vegetable.

If they are pre-germinated, sowing of salsify, scorzonera and parsnip can be postponed until early May, so long as you accept smaller roots – in my view something of an advantage. In this case you can, of course, sow the seeds somewhat closer together than normal – in any case these crops are frequently grown at far too wide a spacing. Grow them in double rows 6 inches (15cm) apart and thus both within the 'fertile band' with the plants staggered 4–6 inches (10–15cm) apart in the rows –

the 6 inch (15cm) spacing will give you larger roots, but fewer of them.

4. Transplanting

When in my book *Composting* I wrote about the best way to transplant I did so a little nervously. My method seemed unnecessarily elaborate when I recollected the way I had seen Cornish broccoli growers doing the job on their steeply sloping fields, a canvas bag of transplants slung round their necks, their right hand grasping the Cornish 'viskie' (the universal Cornish handtool which consists of a 3 foot shaft on the end of which is a moderately heavy blade like a flat part of a mattock), and their left hand plunging into the bag to pull out one bare-root transplant. It is a slow steady rhythmic motion which they can keep up all day without remission – or could, I should say, for this was thirty years ago. Down comes the right hand, the viskie slices into the soil to make a 6 inch (15cm) hole or slit, round comes the left hand to pop the transplant into the slit, forward comes the right foot to bring its iron-tipped heel down on the precise spot to ram the soil hard onto the plant, up follows the left foot, and then again, down comes the viskie, round comes the left hand with the next transplant, and so on. So simple, so quick in spite of the slow even rhythm, and so effective – in those days Cornish broccoli hogged the market from January to June and every evening the 'broccoli express' left Penzance station for the overnight journey to London's Covent Garden market.

Was there something a bit extreme and even absurd in the rather elaborate procedure I advocated? I tended to do my transplanting in the early hours of the morning when I would be safe from the curious questions of passers-by. I felt mildly reassured when the coalman made an approving remark about the

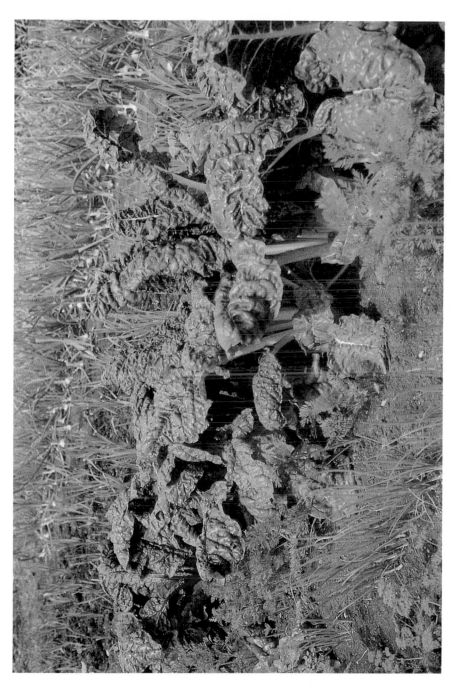

Ruby Swiss chard, a red variety of chard (or seakale beet) is well worth growing. Plant 12 inches (30cm) apart in rich soil to produce tender succulent leaves.

The compost bin – an invaluable part of any organic vegetable garden.

Using compost in the vegetable garden. All vegetables will benefit from the extra nutrients and texture compost gives the soil.

Working in the vegetable garden.

size of my sprouts and when my 7 and 8lb winter cauliflowers gained a small local renown. Then on an autumn holiday in Italy I looked over a wall and saw a gardener planting out finocchio almost exactly in the way I had described. On subsequent enquiry I learned that this method is common practice not only in Italy but in France, too, and I felt vindicated. So I have no hesitation in recommending it here too.

The first factor in transplanting is the quality of the transplant. If you buy them in a garden shop they are mostly 'bare-root' plants – that is they have been pulled straight out of the ground with little or usually no soil attached and often not a lot of root either; or in some cases they consist of a dozen plants grown in peat in one of those 6 by 2 inch (15 by 5cm) plastic troughs. But they, too, are grown so closely that the roots are all entangled together and the process of disentangling them makes them also bare-root and often no-root transplants. Another difficulty is that shop plants are normally only available for a very short period at the traditional planting time (Brussels sprouts the first fortnight in June, and so on) and if you miss them then you have had it.

These two factors make it almost essential for you to grow your own plants, and we should give some attention to this. Most people create a permanent seedbed where all seeds are sown. This means that the brassicas which are the plants grown in seedbeds more than any others will be grown year after year in the same place and will therefore be very liable to disease. By this means a disease contracted in the seedbed could be spread all over the garden. I prefer, where possible, to start winter plants in the same rows as they are going to be grown to maturity. To take an example, we have decided to grow two half rows of purple sprouting broccoli, a total row length of 30 feet (9.15m). If you put your plants 2½ feet (76cm) apart you will need twelve plants. I suggest that you grow your transplants a minimum of 5 inches (12.5cm) apart. This means that, roughly speaking, you need a 5 foot (1.5m) row (or a 2½ foot (76cm) double row) of seedlings later thinned to twelve plants – though to be on the safe side it would be wiser to grow sixteen plants to choose from in a 7 foot (2.1m) row.

The aim is to transplant these plants with a minimum check to growth. First, it is a good idea to mark off the final plant stations with little sticks before you start. Then *thoroughly* water your row of transplants. Next dig at each station a hole about 8 inches (20cm) in depth and across the top. Leave the excavated soil in a neat pile beside the hole – it will come in handy later on for earthing up. Fill the holes with water and let it drain away. If the weather and soil are very dry it is worth doing this twice. Then fill the hole with well-matured compost and stamp the compost down – hard if you are planting brassicas such as sprouts or cauliflowers. You will need a second fill-up to bring the surface level. Replace the little stick in the centre of each hole so that you will not lose track of where it is – which is surprisingly easy to do if, as is sensible, you make and fill up all the holes before proceeding any further. Then make a second lot of holes in the compost, this time trowel-sized (4–5 inches 10–12cm). If the compost is at all dry once again fill each hole with water and let it drain – which will probably take quite a long time. Then lift the transplants one at a time with the trowel, bringing a 4–5 inch (10–12cm) cube of soil attached to the roots of each one. Place this in the hole and push down hard so that the lowest leaves are level with the soil. Ram the soil really hard around them.

Of course, where the seed row is you will already have plants growing in two or three of the final stations. These may be left *in situ* without transplanting, but do not forget that they may be less deeply and less firmly rooted than the others and so may require substantial earthing up or staking. But growing them in this way alongside the transplanted plants will provide you with an interesting comparison between the two methods and, perhaps, help you to decide whether transplanting is beneficial or detrimental to crop production – an issue on which opinions differ.

In the case of brassicas it is advisable to provide some protection against cabbage root fly. You can buy brassica collars, but these are usually made of rather thin material and I prefer to make something a bit more substantial. The best material is old carpet cut into 10 or 12 inch (25–30cm) squares. In the centre make a hole using a heated poker, and then make a slit from the centre to one of the edges with a knife or scalpel. Slide this along the surface so that the plant stem is in the hole in the middle. It is an advantage to have the soil well wetted when you put the squares in position. If you do not have any old carpets to carve up, use several thicknesses of newspaper, preferably with the centre fold along one edge (so as to stop it blowing about). This will not only prevent cabbage root fly, but will also provide a mulch to keep down weeds and prevent the soil drying out. To finish the whole operation sprinkle a 1 inch (2cm) layer of dry earth over the whole row. It is a very good idea, during the summer when the soil is very dry, to bag up a supply of dry soil for use on such occasions. The advantage of a mulch of dry soil is that it, too, acts as

an additional protection against drying out.

The method described above will enable you to plant out sprouts, cauliflowers and purple sprouting broccoli up to late July, and other brassicas correspondingly later. The main danger to watch for is that the cabbage root fly may attack the seed rows. If there are signs of this (plants suddenly wilting, and little whitish-yellow grubs among the roots) you must take immediate counter-measures – refer to a good gardening book such as Lawrence Hills' *Organic Gardening* or *Know and Grow Vegetables*. If you are in an area that is susceptible to attack by cabbage root fly you may have to protect your seed beds from May onwards. One way to do this is to space your seedlings widely enough to enable you to slip a brassica collar or carpet square on them at that stage, which you can later transfer with them when you transplant.

There is another problem which may strike you forcibly the first time you attempt this method, and which may have struck the alert reader already. If you look back to Figure 13, you will see a plan of your sprout and broccoli rows at planting time. The circles represent crops already growing, the crosses mark the stations for your sprouts. The puzzle is to work out how you are going to gain access to these in order to carry out these various earthworks. My answer could be – that is your problem, not mine: you cannot expect to have every operation presented to you on a plate. But seriously, it is a real problem which may partly explain why most gardeners seem to prefer over-wide spacing and are not prone to intercropping. But it is not an insurmountable problem. For example, in the situation illustrated in Figure 13, you will at this time be harvesting your intercropping lettuces and cabbages, and you should try to lift first those plants that will be in the way. I have lightly shaded those I would lift first. If you look at the diagram of the whole garden (Figure 14) you will see that row 9a (purple sprouting broccoli) is accessible from the 9a/10a space; for access to row 9b you must sow and pick your spring onions so as to leave spaces in appropriate places; similarly, 7b and 8b can be made accessible by gaps in your radishes. Of course, as soon as the brassicas are planted and no longer in need of attention, you can make further sowings of onions and radishes which will be needed anyway for later on in the summer. So, like many problems, it is not insoluble, but only requires a little advance thought.

If you are planting out leeks (or any crop where plants are grown fairly close together) it is hardly practicable to use this method. In the case of leeks I think there are three things to be said: first, do not plant them too deep and, thus, below the most fertile 4–6 inches (10–15cm) of the topsoil; secondly, plant them in a shallow trench that has been well composted – normally, of course, in the fertile band; thirdly, plant them close together in a double row, each plant 7 inches (17.5cm) from its neighbour, and be satisfied with smaller but more numerous plants. The total weight of crop will be roughly the same. Take care when sowing seeds to space them well apart and then thin the plants to 1–2 inches (2.5–5cm) apart (this means you should sow three 5 foot (1.5m) rows 3 inches (7.5cm) apart in the seedbed to produce enough plants for a double 30 foot (9.15m) row). One reason why leeks normally need to be planted out early is that seedlings are grown so bunched together that they do not have a chance to grow.

This is, I think, the moment to consider one further factor in the performance of our crops – that is, the distance between adjacent rows and the distance between plants in the rows. We are concentrating our manure and compost in the 'fertile band' roughly 11 inches (28cm) wide and it is important that as many of our heavy feeders are planted within this band as possible. Most of the winter crops we dealt with in the last chapter were plants which would eventually grow very large and were planted, therefore, in a single row in the centre of the band, and for which very generous composting provision was made when planting them out. What about those much smaller crops which are customarily planted closer together, often in double or triple rows? Here is a list of the more common ones:

	Distance apart of rows (in inches)	Distance apart of plants in row (in inches)
Broad bean	8	8
Beetroot	10	5
Spinach beet	15	9
Carrot	10	6
Celery	15	12
Kohlrabi	12	12
Leek	12	6
Lettuce	12	8
Onions	12	6
Parsnip	12	10
Salsify	12	12
Scorzonera	12	12
Swede	12	12
Turnip	12	6

These distances between rows and plants represent a rough average of three or four spacings that are recommended. In various books the figures given differ quite a lot – in fact, the whole question of the distances between plants and rows seems quite arbitrary: recommendations for turnips, for example, vary between 'plant 6 inches apart in rows 12 inches apart'

Figure 17: Various ways of spacing turnip plants in rows

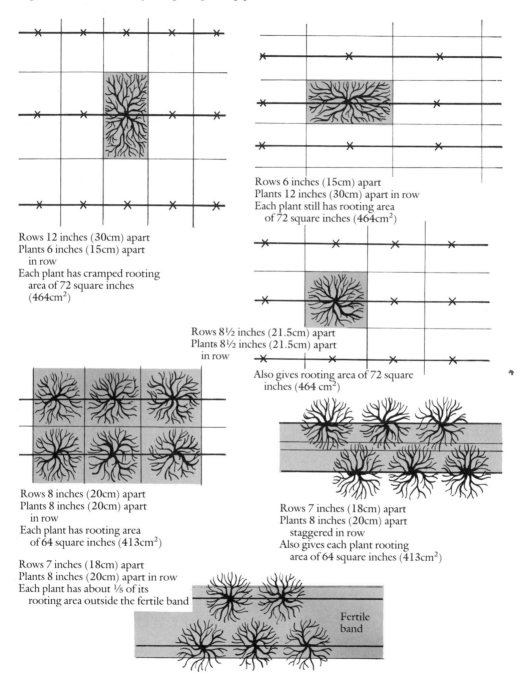

Rows 12 inches (30cm) apart
Plants 6 inches (15cm) apart
    in row
Each plant has cramped rooting
    area of 72 square inches
    (464cm²)

Rows 6 inches (15cm) apart
Plants 12 inches (30cm) apart in row
Each plant still has rooting area
    of 72 square inches (464cm²)

Rows 8½ inches (21.5cm) apart
Plants 8½ inches (21.5cm) apart
    in row
Also gives rooting area of 72 square
    inches (464 cm²)

Rows 8 inches (20cm) apart
Plants 8 inches (20cm) apart
    in row
Each plant has rooting area
    of 64 square inches (413cm²)

Rows 7 inches (18cm) apart
Plants 8 inches (20cm) apart
staggered in row
Also gives each plant rooting
    area of 64 square inches (413cm²)

Rows 7 inches (18cm) apart
Plants 8 inches (20cm) apart in row
Each plant has about ⅕ of its
    rooting area outside the fertile band

Fertile
band

and 'plants 12 inches apart and rows 18 inches apart' – that is between 72 square inches per plant and 216 square inches, three times as much. If we accepted the figures given above as they stand we would hardly be able to fit any double rows within our fertile band. So spurred on by necessity and a modicum of common sense let us look more closely at the distances usually recommended.

The first point to strike one is that as far as space for the plant is concerned it does not really make any difference whether plants are, say, 6 inches apart in rows 12 inches apart, or 12 inches apart in rows 6 inches apart. In either case they will have available roughly 72 square inches of space for their roots and their leaves. As far as our fertile band goes we would not gain anything by planting them 12 inches apart in 6 inch rows as against having a single row 6 inches apart – we would still only get thirty turnips in our 15 foot row.

However, let us explore further. You will see from Figure 17 that whichever way we grow turnips (or most of the other vegetables on the list) their root run will be squashed in – it is a narrow oval rather than a circle. I think that even without investigating or testing it, it is a fair assumption that plants would be likely to benefit by having an equal root-run in all directions. This seems common sense and yet generation after generation has meekly accepted the universally recommended procedure of widely-spaced rows with close planting within the rows. This shows, I think, how important it is to question age-old habits and accepted wisdom, and it is strange that it took a highly specialized research scientist (Dr J. K. A. Bleasdale, Director of the National Vegetable Research Station and co-editor and author of the book *Know and Grow Vegetables*) to point such an obvious

fact out, and all gardeners must be indebted to him and his colleagues for the new light they have thrown on this and other gardening matters. This chapter, in particular, owes a debt to *Know and Grow Vegetables*.

So, there are two important factors as regards spacing, and these have to be balanced against such points as the size of the beds, the convenience of the rows, access, cultivation (for example, hoeing between the rows) and so on – and, of course, in our case taking maximum advantage of our fertile row. These factors are:

1. The number of plants that will grow in a given area, that is to say how much total space a plant needs.
2. Generally speaking it is preferable for plants to be equidistant from their neighbours in all directions so that they may have equal root-run all round.

I should add that not all plants do better with equal spacing and until a lot more have been systematically tested we shall not know which benefit and which do not. But as far as can be seen, no plants do worse with it so the safest bet is to aim for equal spacing where it does not conflict with other requirements. In our case a major requirement is to accommodate as many of our main winter vegetables within the fertile band as possible. Luckily the trend nowadays is towards closer planting and smaller, but more numerous, crops.

The 12 inch (30cm) row distance which is so common has crept in by tradition, perhaps as a matter of convenience for the tools used on commercial holdings; perhaps quite simply because a foot is a length that comes to mind quite naturally. At any rate there is no logic to justify it for allotments or kitchen gardens.

Table 4: Revised distances for planting crops staggered in the rows

	Distance apart of rows		Distance apart of plants in rows, staggered
Broad beans	7 in (18cm)	10 in (25cm)	
Beetroot	7 in (18cm)	7 in (18cm)	
Spinach, and seakale beet	7 in (18cm)	10 in (25cm)	
Celery			Single row (trying to squeeze in two rows less than 8 inches (20cm) apart does not pay off, especially if you have to go to the expense of buying plants.)
Carrot	3.5 in (9cm)	3.5 in (9cm)	Triple row (or you could have four rows only 3 inches (7cm) apart, the outer one 1 inch (2.5cm) from the edge of the band).
Kohlrabi	7 in (18cm)	10 in (25cm)	
Leek	7 in (18cm)	7 in (18cm)	(or 10 inches (25cm) if prefer larger leeks.)
Lettuce	7 in (18cm)	10 in (25cm)	For large hearting lettuces. Smaller varieties such as little Gem can be grown in triple rows 4 inches (10cm) apart – however these lettuces will not normally be grown in the fertile row.
Onion	7 in (18cm)	3.5–7 in (19–18cm)	Depending on whether you prefer small or large onions.
Parsnip	7 in (18cm)	4–8 in (10–20cm)	Depending on whether you prefer small or large parsnips.
Salsify Scorzonera	7 in (18cm)	4–6 in (10–15cm)	
Swede	7 in (18cm)	20 in (51cm)	Better than having a single row at 12 inch (30cm) spacing, giving you twenty swedes in a double row rather than fifteen in a single row
Turnip	7 in (18cm)	8 in (20cm)	

So, returning to our turnips, to achieve this equal root-run the plants must be placed so that they are equidistant in every direction, that is 8½ inches apart in rows 8½ inches apart, which gives 72 square inches per plant, within which the roots will, roughly speaking, occupy a circle of diameter 8½ inches. However, the fact that we have now given the plants a better deal means that they probably will not require quite so much total root-run as when they were all squashed up, so we can cut them down to 8 inches apart in rows 8 inches apart: that is a circular root-run of 8 inches diameter. This is some

improvement in spacing, but you can achieve a further economy of space if you stagger the plants in each row so that the plants in one row grow opposite the spaces in the adjacent row. This will mean that the top of the circular root-run in the second row will fit between the bottoms of those in the first row. This will enable us to bring the rows a little closer together without having to diminish the 8 inch diameter root-run.

Without going into complicated calculations, this can be achieved by having the plants 8 inches apart in rows 7 inches apart, staggered in the rows, which will bring each plant 2 inches from the edge of the fertile band each side, and you will get forty-four plants in a 15 foot row instead of thirty.

We could therefore re-write the list of plants on page 67 with revised distances for planting them staggered in the rows, so that we can grow the double rows between the fertile band (see Table 4).

I think that if you are fairly assiduous in practising the methods outlined in this chapter – even if you only practise some of them – you will have no difficulty in adhering to the plan in the last chapter, and probably improving on it, even if you live in the North of England. You will, perhaps, be tempted to try to fit in more plantings, but I think you should resist trying to be too ambitious initially. Things never work out quite as planned: there might be a deluge of rain, so the seeds do not germinate and have to be re-sown; or an invasion of slugs might decimate your crops; a late frost cuts back your potatoes; the cat from next door . . . . well, there is no need for me to spell out all the potential hazards of gardening – the golden rule is to leave yourself a reasonable amount of leeway.

CHAPTER 6
MANURING AND COMPOSTING

In the last chapter I wrote of improving performance by planning the use of your ground more efficiently so that space and growing time are both used to maximum advantage. In this chapter I shall consider improving performance by making your soil effectively more fertile. Making the most of whatever manure, compost and fertilizer you have available may seem a far cry from planning, but it is a major factor in the success of your garden, and this will be affected by the way you plan its use.

The soil loses its fertility in two principal ways: first, by the fact that you are taking crops off it, and that these crops are removing from the soil the nutrients and the organic matter which the soil has contributed to their growth; and second, by the fact that even if you do not grow crops in the soil there will be a natural process of depletion by weathering, leaching and bacterial action. These losses of fertility must be made good; indeed, as many gardens and allotments exist in a state of comparatively low productivity, their fertility needs to be built up over the years.

Your planning must take into account three main factors about organic fertilizers – and here I am speaking mainly about organics because fertilizers out of a bag do not affect planning very much. Generally speaking, chemical fertilizers are water-soluble and they leach out of the soil within a season and do not make any long-term contribution to fertility.

1. As I have already mentioned there is never nearly enough fertilizer. For example, it is frequently recommended that land should be manured before planting peas and beans; in the case of a strict rotation this means that each section is manured once in three or four years (depending whether it is a 3- or 4-year rotation). But this is not really good enough as it would not maintain the fertility of an already fertile garden, let alone build up that of an infertile one. There is a widely held belief that although the effect of chemical fertilizers is transient, that of organic fertilizers lasts almost indefinitely. This is a much exaggerated viewpoint. As soon as an organic fertilizer is applied, the microbiological population will be at work using the carbohydrate component as energy, and converting the complex organic molecules into simpler inorganic ones, so that even if no crops are grown the humus and nutrient content of the soil is being dissipated. Donald Hopkins in his book *Chemicals, Humus and the Soil* estimates that the main effects of an application of organic fertilizer to the soil are more or less exhausted within nine months – though this does not take into account the long-term effects

on the basic structure of the soil.

2. Manure is best used when thoroughly broken down, preferably in a compost heap. Again, there is some disagreement about this and I would say from observation that the majority of gardeners disagree, or at any rate do not carry it into practice. They spread manure, either freshly in the autumn, or partially decomposed in the spring, directly on their garden. Those who practise what used to be called 'bastard' trenching will incorporate it with weeds at the bottom of the top spit – though this practice is becoming rarer. Sometimes they will mix it roughly into the top spit of the soil, often using one of the small garden rotovators for the purpose; and sometimes they will spread it over the whole garden as a mulch. This is not the place to go into the pros and cons of direct application versus composting – they are discussed in my book *Composting*. But there is one good argument in favour of composting: manure has a high proportion of nitrogen as compared with carbon – in fact, it has an excess of nitrogen which will be wasted either by leaching or by escaping as a gas (hence the strong smell of ammonia, which is a chemical combination of nitrogen and hydrogen, in the vicinity of fresh farmyard manure); garden weeds and rubbish generally have a much higher proportion of carbon which makes it very slow and difficult to break down into compost on its own. But if the two are mixed together the nitrogen in the manure will behave as an activator for the weeds and you will get maximum benefits from the combination of the two. As a result, of course, you will have more and better organic material available for use than you will by using them separately.

3. To get the best out of compost it should be applied to plants when and where they are growing – it is a waste to use it as a general mulch or to spread it over the whole plot indiscriminately or to apply it where there is no crop to reap immediate benefit from it. As many of the plants it is providing for in the fertile row will be comparatively deep-rooted, incorporate the compost for them into the top 8 inches (20cm) of the soil or deeper – for some crops like winter celery which are grown in a trench you may be composting to a depth of 12 inches (30cm) below the surface.

There is a fourth factor about manure which it is as well to be aware of. How serious it is, is open to question and a matter of personal choice. This factor is that in most cases the only manure easily available to you will come from intensive pig or poultry units. In these units animals are subjected to a variety of hormone and chemical treatments to stimulate growth. Of course, on a practical level we can comfort ourselves that most (though not all) of these contaminants are excreted – but they are not necessarily lost, for they are then recycled into the soil as manure. This worries those people who know, for example, that excessive trace elements, such as copper, in the soil will inhibit plant growth, and they will also be taken up by some plants and thus become a possibly harmful ingredient of food.

Since 95 per cent of all the eggs, chickens and pig meat we eat now comes from these intensive units presumably most of us are not too worried about the quality of the manure we buy

– for nearly 100 per cent of the manure available to us comes from intensive units – unless we can find a supply of horse manure. If you belong to the minority who does not fancy using products that you suspect may be contaminated, or of using products that are associated with intensive farming, then probably your only reliable source of manure is your local stables. Or you may live near enough the coast to make collecting large amounts of seaweed a possibility. Seaweed is an excellent organic fertilizer and is also useful as a compost activator. The third, and perhaps the best alternative is your own urine (and, where possible, that of your family and visitors). There is no danger from bacteria or other infection but there is a problem with waterlogging and also, of course, with prying neighbours!

Otherwise you may have to use a proprietary brand of compost maker or, probably as good and far cheaper, a chemical nitrogen fertilizer to activate your compost heap. A possible alternative is the use of green manure crops and this is dealt with in Chapter 7.

Compost or composted manure serves four main purposes: it improves or maintains the physical structure and quality of the soil; it helps the soil to retain moisture; it darkens the soil which enables it to absorb and retain more of the heat of the sun; and it provides nutrients – in particular a slow steady flow of available nitrogen, as complex proteins in the organic material are converted by bacteria into soluble nitrates. This process goes on anyway, even if the nutrients are not taken up by the plants, in which case they will be released into the atmosphere or leached away into water courses. Although the soil improvement will to some extent remain and will build up over time if the process is repeated year after year, the availability of nutrients will reduce through the season as the compost is mineralized by the action of bacteria. I used to think this happened mainly during the warmth of the summer months when bacterial activity is at its greatest, which perhaps did not matter too much as there are usually enough crops or weeds growing at that time to take up the nutrients as they are released (as well as contributing to the growth of the crops, by contributing to the weeds they will be preserved for future composting and recycling). But I recently read of some research which claimed that organic growers are as much to blame for the nitrification of water courses as users of chemical fertilizers because of their habit of spreading compost and manure in the autumn. Bacteria convert the insoluble nitrogen compounds into water-soluble nitrates over the winter and as there are few or no crops growing to take these up, and plenty of rain to wash them away, the nitrate leaches into the water courses. Well, I do not know how true this is, but it does seem to suggest two things: that some, at least, of the value of organic fertilizers can be wasted if you spread them wholesale in the autumn (as is so often recommended); and second, that a soil loses some of its goodness over the winter if there are no crops growing on it to take up the nutrients as they become available (as is also often recommended 'for letting the frost get to it'). This, too, is dealt with further in Chapter 7.

So the rule is mature your compost well so that it is fully decomposed, and then concentrate it on the plants that are greedy for it and put it on when they need it – that is, when they are eager to grow. This means we are talking about applying it in the spring and summer, and principally to the crops such as:

Brassicas, especially sprouts, cauliflowers and broccoli
Potatoes
Celery and celeriac
Leek
Pea and bean, especially runner and climbing beans
Marrow, sweet corn

These are just the vegetables we have discussed growing in our main 'fertile rows'. So, it is the fertile rows that you are going to be feeding year after year, building up their organic content, and it is here that you will be growing most of the crops which really need and demand organic matter. Thus, one of the major benefits claimed for this system of planning is that your heavy feeders are always grown in the same 'fertile belt' and, therefore, the majority of your manuring, composting, fertilizing and soil improvement can be concentrated in this area.

I say 'soil improvement' and this is a subject that needs a mention. Most of these crops are heavy feeders, and also deep rooters, and it is important to make sure that they are able to benefit from their deep-rooting systems. Most people are aware that heavy clay soils become compacted and that even if they are opened up on the surface they may remain compacted below, often providing a layer that is almost impervious to drainage and to root penetration. This has already been mentioned on page 17 and I think it needs looking into a little further. What people are not so aware of (and nor was I until recently, when I moved to East Anglia) is that a loose, sandy, almost dusty soil can suffer from the same complaint. Many sandy soils are a mixture of coarse sand, fine sand and silt. When the soil is worked and disturbed by digging, cropping and general cultivation, it dries out and becomes dusty. On seeing this dusty,

sandy surface one assumes that this is an 'open' soil, that this condition continues indefinitely and that one's main problem will be watering and leaching and maintaining the humus level. This is not always so: below the level at which it is normally worked, this kind of soil may compact into a hard rock-like substance which it requires all one's strength to penetrate. Yet if you bring this material to the surface the lumps will quite easily break up into their components of sand and silt. What appears to happen is that over the years the small particles of sand and silt wedge more and more tightly in the spaces between the larger particles causing the whole to lock together into an impenetrable layer.

The modern tendency is to cultivate the ground much more shallowly than in the past, even among people who are not no-diggers. The small rotovators that you often see on allotments hardly go down more than 6 or 8 inches below the surface, and few people dig deeper than a spade's depth. The soil 8 inches (20cm) below the surface often remains undisturbed indefinitely, compacting away over the years. No-diggers work on the theory that if they provide enough organic matter spread on the surface or in the topsoil the worms will carry it down and do their cultivation for them, but suppose the worms cannot penetrate the subsoil either? I also question how much organic material over a long period of time is needed to breed and feed enough worms to have enough effect to bring this underground layer into a state of effective fertility?

I was brought up on double digging, or double trenching as it was called then, which meant digging down two spits deep. The alternative for lazy gardeners was 'bastard trenching', where you dug down one spit and merely loosened the soil in the second spit. Nowadays we tend not even to do that, but merely to stir around the top spit.

When I first learned of the no-digging technique shortly after the Second World War, I felt this was a major breakthrough in the history of human endeavour and that gardening would no longer involve those weary hours of double digging every year as the dark dank days of winter overtook us. Now, forty years later this hard rock-like subsoil of East Anglia has caused me to have second thoughts. I still believe that no-digging is a practicable idea and that when it is possible it is a very good method of cultivation. But it is not a universal cure-all and one has to fit one's practice to one's soil and situation and not use it blindly where it is not appropriate. No-digging requires a soil with a very high organic content, well irrigated, with an acidity that never strays far below neutral, and to whose surface you can year after year continue to apply substantial quantities of organic matter. If you take over an allotment or garden that is not in this condition or near it, it may take several years to reach it. By 'several years' I mean probably a minimum of five years of very heavy manuring or composting – and where in East Anglia (or elsewhere) can you get this sort of quantity of manure that is not heavily contaminated with the results of intensive pig and poultry units and pesticides? I have mentioned horse-manure and seaweed, but even seaweed has to be regarded with some reservations for no-diggers. I remember examining the soil in the Scilly Isles where seaweed has been used liberally for centuries. The soil there is obviously extremely fertile but as far as I could see it had almost no worms in it at all – presumably the continual applications of salt in the seaweed has turned the soil into a hostile environment in which

worms could not survive. So who is going to carry out the cultivation for the no-diggers? Of course, in theory, you can hose the salt out of the seaweed, but this presupposes a lot of space, a yard where the water can run away and where it is practicable to make a lot of mess, and, of course, quite a lot of time to carry out this operation. Another consideration is where you collect seaweed from: I would advise, to be on the safe side, avoiding seaweed from the Cumbrian coast as this may well have been contaminated by outfalls from the nuclear power stations in the vicinity. Similarly, it would be wise not to use seaweed from other such sites around the country.

I think that in the early stages it is quite important to reassure yourself at regular intervals that your fertile strip is fertile for two spits deep, which will involve examining it every few years to ascertain its condition. Dig up a spadeful of this sub-soil and examine it: is it hard, impervious? Does it have any roots in it, or worm-runs or cracks? Is there any sign of organic matter in it? If you practise a four-year rotation it is a good plan to examine one plot a year, so that each plot is examined and treated once in four years. If it shows signs of compaction or infertility (I am talking about the second spit down, remember) then it needs treatment. Do not let this daunt you too much for I am referring here only to the 'fertile band' and this comprises less than a third of your garden. The best method I have found is the following (see Figure 18):

First, dig out the top spit for about 5 feet (1.5m) and pile it on one side of the row, making the trench about 11 inches (27.5cm) wide. Then dig out the second spit and put it on the other side. You are now 15–18 inches (37.5–45cm) below the level of the surface. If it is still hard (and, of course, it is likely

Figure 18: Double digging

Topsoil   Row being trenched   Second spit

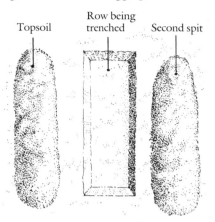

1 Dig out two spits deep, depositing soil each side of the trench

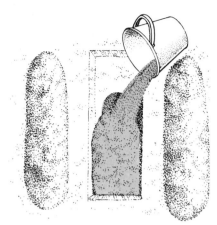

2 Add one bucketful of rough compost and fork it in

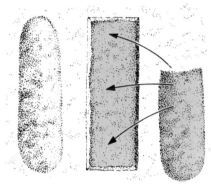

3 Replace part of second spit and spread in trench

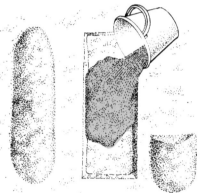

4 Add 2–3 bucketfuls of compost, spread and mix with the loose soil

5 Continue, leaving a small amount of soil to add to your reserve of soil

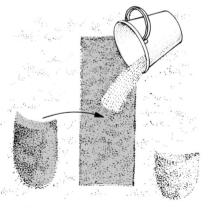

6 Continue with the topsoil pile until it and the reserve are all used up

to be) stir the soil for a further few inches. If it is very hard it is difficult to know which tools to recommend for all this. I am the lucky possessor of a heavy narrow curved trenching spade; half a dozen lunges with this will usually break through the hardest soil. But having recently broken the handle of an ordinary spade I am fearful of breaking this one too, and I always have a 4 foot (1.2m) crowbar handy as well; and, of course, a long-pronged pickaxe is also a useful tool.

Then empty into the trench about one full bucket of compost over the whole 5 foot (1.5m) length. I usually have a special compost heap for very coarse materials – chopped up brassica stalks, coarse grass, old strawberry plants, soft hedge-trimmings, etc. This I usually leave undisturbed for eighteen months or so. By the end of this time it will have largely decomposed, though it will still be pretty rough. In taking it out I slice down the face of it with a sharpened spade, putting on one side any really hard material and edges that have dried out, and use them to start the next heap.

I mix this rough compost with the loose soil in the bottom of the trench. Then I put in several buckets of the subsoil followed by another bucket of the compost and so on – the proportion of subsoil to compost I use depends on how much compost I have and feel I can spare. If it is all pretty dry – and in recent years on the east coast of Britain even the subsoil at 18 inches (45cm) down has been very dry indeed – I water it down with two gallons of water to every 5 feet. I do not honestly know how useful this is; I just feel it may help the bacteria to get to work homogenizing these two layers, one of quite rich, organic soil and the other of pretty arid, barren subsoil. Then I replace the topsoil. I may put some compost with

the topsoil too – this will depend upon its general condition, what crops are to follow, etc. If I did I would not use compost from the 'rough heap' but from the main heap that I endeavour to make reasonably fine and homogeneous. I would also, of course, not be likely to put it on in the autumn (and this trenching operation is most likely to take place in the autumn) unless I had planned for autumn crops to follow.

This trenching process does involve quite a lot of earthworks and you may find yourself limited for space. One possibility is to put the top soil you dig out on the side where there is most room and to put the first 5 feet (1.5m) of the subsoil into a wheelbarrow or a bag (a 1 cwt (50kg) fertilizer bag will just about take it). Then, instead of replacing the soil, start the next 5 feet of row and throw the subsoil from that row into the first 5 feet (1.5m) of trench. Then mix it with the rough compost as you go and finish off by replacing the top soil on top of it. Then proceed down the row in similar manner and when you come to the last five feet (1.5m) fetch the bag or barrow of original subsoil and use that (see Figure 19).

By this time you will find your soil level has risen by several inches – and it is, in fact, by a similar method that practitioners of raised bed systems create their raised beds. If you want to keep your beds level, it is quite useful to dispose of some of this soil (preferably the subsoil, not the composted soil) in a heap – I find it very useful to have a heap of soil available for such jobs as earthing up, topping off a compost heap, filling in holes, etc.

All this may seem quite an undertaking and not at all your idea of fun gardening, so let me try to sweeten the pill:

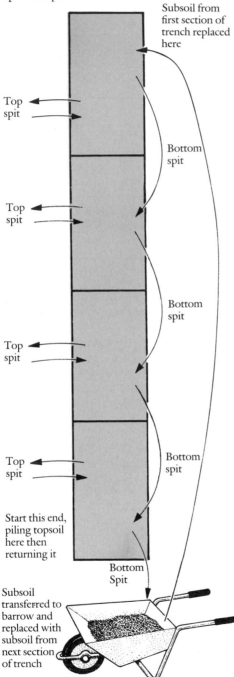

Figure 19: Double digging to break up a hard pan

Subsoil from first section of trench replaced here

Top spit

Bottom spit

Top spit

Bottom spit

Top spit

Bottom spit

Top spit

Bottom spit

Start this end, piling topsoil here then returning it

Bottom Spit

Subsoil transferred to barrow and replaced with subsoil from next section of trench

1. You only ever have to do it if your subsoil is in bad shape.
2. If you do have to do it, and make a good job of it, you may never have to do it again.
3. In any case, you are only likely to have to do it a maximum of once in every four years, that is to one plot each year, and then only in the fertile rows. This means that in the allotment we have been considering you would only have to trench six 15 foot (4.5m) rows each year

Of course, there is nothing to stop you giving the same treatment to the whole of your garden, rather than to just the fertile rows, and obviously it would be beneficial to do so. And if your intercropping rows are not doing well you may have no option. Again the same rule applies – concentrate the greater part of your energies and resources on the fertile rows, but do not forget that doing this must operate at the expense of the rest of your garden.

I have now started a routine of carrying out this check on the subsoil every autumn on the pea and bean plot. The reason for choosing this plot is that it is the one time when the land is likely to be clear of crops. Also in a four-year rotation the peas and beans are followed by root crops which more than any other will be pleased to find nice loose friable soil below, and will reward you correspondingly. There is a heresy about roots that has taken deep root in the minds of gardeners that you should not apply compost to root crops. This is mistaken. What is true is that they do not respond to a top spit that consists of very rough immature compost; and from this has spread the idea that they should not be given any form of organic matter. This is quite untrue: they thrive on it – though it does depend upon the quality of the compost. In fact, one of the best ways of growing parsnips or salsify – indeed, the only way of growing them well in stony or clayey soil – is to make conical holes with a crowbar and fill them with fine compost. When you come to lift the crop you will find each root almost exactly fitting the hole you have made. It is as if the cone of soil had been miraculously transmuted into parsnip, and this is indeed what has happened. The weeds, trimmings, roots, stalks and manure that you put on your compost heap have, over a period of one season, and through several intermediate trans-formations, returned to your dining table, *mirabile dictu*, as a dish of delectable and nutritious vegetables.

There is another rather similar myth that has grown up: you should not apply compost or manure in the same season as you apply lime. Yes, this is so if you are digging in raw manure which contains nitrogen in the form of ammo-nia. If you apply this manure and lime together they will react chemically, and the nitrogen will be released as a gas and will be lost in the atmosphere. This will only occur with fresh manure; in compost or composted manure the ammonia will have been converted to other forms (proteins, nitrates, etc.) which will not react with the lime.

As a result of these two myths we are often advised to apply manure to the pea and bean plot in preference to the others. On the contrary, I would reverse this advice: if you do happen to be short of manure this is the plot I would be inclined to pass over. The reason is, as I have mentioned earlier, that peas and beans and legumes generally which, as you will remember, are our nitrogen fixers, have a lazy, self-indulgent dis-position in their natures: so long as there is plenty of nitrogen in the soil they do not fix it themselves, they just rely on what is there. It does, therefore, seem a pity to apply nitrogenous composts just when they will reduce the activities of our friendly, unpaid, organic-nitrogen-providers.

So the answer is, stick to mature or composted manure and put it on when you please, preferably every year on the fertile band. And every fourth year (or probably more conveniently, a quarter of your plot every year) test your subsoil and, if necessary, dig into it some rough compost.

Before we close this chapter we must look at the area between the fertile band where our intercropping rows will grow. We have off and on paid lip-service to its needs but have tended to treat it in a rather cavalier fashion. This is as it should be. A garden is like a communist utopia: from each according to its ability, to each according to its needs. After all, if the needs of the brassicas and winter crops are great so, too, is the reward they offer when in the dark drear days of January and February it is the succession of sprouts which keeps us going; and as soon as they are over the first presage of spring is heralded with an array of great creamy cauliflowers suddenly appearing almost overnight like a miracle. Compost is too precious to waste on those with skimpy appetites, when there are these gour-mands and gluttons around on whom it can be lavished. Lettuce, spinach, all the summer vegetables do, of course, need and appreciate a good fertile soil, but they are surface rooting – they do not require the depth and quality that the lavish feeders do; unlike the winter vegetables they will produce a worth-while crop without it; and over the years as the fertility of your whole garden increases, they too will have their turn. I do not suggest we should starve them of nutrients; only that we should concentrate our scarce resources where they are most needed rather than spreading them indiscriminately over the whole area.

Of course, books tend to demand that *every* crop requires a deeply dug well-composted site – and this is fine, but they do not say where all this compost is to come from. I am not saying do not compost between the main rows; what I am saying is – make as much compost as you can and be sure that your fertile band has first priority in its use. Keep what you can spare for between these rows, and use it with discrimination. Obviously when you are growing self-blanching celery, or sweet corn or onions, you will need a fertile soil, but it does not have to go very deep. Probably a bucketful for about every three yards (3m) of row is what you should aim for for these and similar crops, though, of course, it varies with the crop: celery would probably need more to be worthwhile growing.

But this will not ensure that your intercropping rows are composted systematically and I think it is important to incorporate some manuring on a regular basis to ensure that these areas are not neglected. I have suggested that your fertile band should be manured (which is a generic term I use for the application of manure, compost or other organic fertilizers such as seaweed) annually if possible, and that much of this should be worked into the soil to a depth of 8 inches (20cm) or more. I suggest that the areas between should be regularly manured all over once every four years (or a quarter of the plot every year). This need not be worked in so deeply as in the fertile band – keep it to the top 4 inches (10cm). This will, of course, be in addition to the extra boosts you apply when growing greedy crops in these areas.

Your fertile band comprises one-third of your garden (11 inches out of 32 inches, or 27cm out of 80cm) but this does not mean that this system provides three times as much compost for this third as spreading compost wholesale would have done because of the need to apply some compost also between the fertile bands. Imagine that you make 6 tons of compost a year. Then reserve 5 cwt (0.254kg) for intercropping plants such as sweet corn, self-blanching celery, etc. Spread 25 cwt (1.27t) wholesale over one plot (a quarter) of the intercropping rows. The remainder (4.5 tons) will go on the fertile bands. This means that the fertile bands will receive well over twice their share of what is going, and the rest will get less than half its fair share. In fact the fertile band will get roughly six times as much compost in proportion as the rest.

To make reasonable compost you need two bins, so that the compost heap may be turned from one bin into the next. For a full allotment (90 feet by 30 feet, 27.5m by 9m) you are really better off with four, but this will take up a lot of room which you may be reluctant to spare. But if you think of that 10 tons of mature compost a season that you need to maintain fertility (not forgetting that initially you are quite likely to have to build the fertility up to this level) you have to calculate how you are going to produce the six or seven binfuls you will need to produce per season. It is perfectly possible to do this with two bins but it will depend on a well-organised process, a very well made heap, a ready supply of manure or some other activator, and at least one turning of each heap to do it. For a half-sized allotment one double bin in the shape of an 'E' should provide 6 tons of compost a year quite easily.

CHAPTER 7
GREEN MANURING

Cultivation of land and the consequent removal of weeds and crops obviously depletes the soil of some of its fertility and nutrients. A portion of this will be returned to the soil if the weeds and unused parts of the crop are composted, and this will leave only the components of the edible portion to be replaced. But, in addition, the soil suffers loss of nutrients because of leaching, though this will be minimized so long as there are plants growing which will absorb them. One of the purposes of bringing in manure and other fertilizers from outside is to replace these losses (the other purpose is to balance the excess carbon in your compost heap and activate its fermentation). How far we could maintain the garden's fertility without importing fertilizer from outside is open to doubt. What is indisputable is that we can make some contribution towards it by utilizing vacant ground to grow green manure crops which can be turned into the soil or preferably used in our compost heaps. Gardeners are unlikely to be willing to forego an edible crop in order to grow a green manure crop, but nearly all gardens have empty spaces from time to time where a crop has been lifted and nothing as yet has replaced it, and often also where the space between crops is empty, for example, between rows of maincrop peas or climbing beans. The aim must be to make full use of this empty land without interfering with crop production.

There is quite a large choice of green manure plants, and there is one important distinction to be made between them. Most plants, if recycled by composting, will increase the fertility of the soil to the extent that all plants extract carbon from the atmosphere and also capture the energy of the sun which provides the fuel for plant growth and store it. All the other components of plants come from the soil in the form of nutrients so even if the whole plant is composted and returned to the soil it does not increase the soil's nutrients – it merely returns what it took out in growing. However, this is a valuable contribution because it conserves the nutrients which would otherwise be leached away, and it also maintains the fertility which otherwise declines naturally.

Those plants which are members of the legume family, however, have an additional bonus. they fix nitrogen from the atmosphere. Other plants do not have this ability (though there is now a suspicion that some other plants do have it to a small degree, and that new varieties could eventually be bred to do so). Peas and beans are legumes and if you examine their roots you will see little white nodules on them. These nodules consist of bacteria which live on the plant and which also have this ability to capture nitrogen which is then used in the plant's growth. If the plants are composted, this additional nitrogen is, of course, incorporated into the compost. These bacteria are specific to the plant (though a few plants such as lucerne and fenugreek are host to the same bacteria) so the plant will not fix nitrogen unless your soil contains the appropriate bacteria. Most soils do contain them, but it is worth checking to see if the nodules are present on your legumes. If they are not, the best thing to do is to try to get hold of one or two plants from other gardens or farms which do have them and which, if planted in your garden, will then spread the bacteria in your soil. Once your soil is populated with the right bacteria it should remain so as long as you continue to grow the host plant. If you are not successful in doing this you had better change to a different green manure crop because, of course, you are not receiving all the benefits you should from this one.

Green manures of this kind, therefore, have the same advantage as manure; they can supply nitrogen in an organic form to balance the excess of carbon in most other garden waste. They can, therefore, be used as activators in the compost heap in the same way as manure can.

The main leguminous green manure plants are:

Vetches (including winter tares)
Clover (including melilot)
Lucerne (alfalfa)
Lupins
Fenugreek
The pea and bean families

Non-leguminous green manures are:
Rye-grass
Buckwheat
Mustard
Comfrey
Fodder radish
Agricultural chicory

Some garden plants are particularly valuable as green manures, and these include: sunflower, sweet corn, Jerusalem artichoke, peas and beans. However do not forget that when a plant is cropped it is to that extent depleting the soil, however much of it is returned to the soil via the compost heap. It is generally considered that there is an advantage in combining two or more crops on the same plot – for example, winter tares and rye-grass, or fenugreek undersown beneath sweet corn. I am not sure whether there is any hard evidence for this but it seems a good idea.

I have not tried all of these green manure plants, and with a few of them I have not had much success, so I will limit myself here to mentioning the ones I have found most useful:

For overwintering:

Winter tares Sow up to September or, if pre-germinated (easy to do as the large seed will be individually sown anyway in drills) mid-October. It will remain quite small throughout the winter but spring into prodigious growth during April and May.

Hungarian rye-grass (also known as *grazing-rye*) Sow up to September or, if pre-germinated, mid-October. Makes a large bulk of material by the following May. A mixture of rye-grass and tares is a good combination.

Broad bean ⎫ These are
Tic, daffa or *winter beans* ⎭ very similar from the green manure point of view, except that broad bean seed is more expensive (though you can save the seed from the rows you sow for cropping). Sow up to the end of November to produce green manure by the end of May. This is quite a separate

planting from the broad beans you grow for food. It is useful for following maincrop potatoes or other late crops. All beans are, of course, nitrogen fixers.

Quick maturing summer green manure:
   Mustard Will produce a massive growth within eight weeks. However, it is a brassica so it should only be used in the cabbage/cauliflower plot if you are practising a rotation.
   Fenugreek Will mature in ten to twelve weeks. It is a legume so it will fix nitrogen. However, if it has never been grown before in your garden your soil may not contain the appropriate bacteria for nitrogen fixing, which you can recognize by the fact that no small nodules grow on the fenugreek roots. In this case, obtain a plant or so of lucerne from a friendly farmer and plant it amongst your fenugreek. If left, the fenugreek will seed itself.
   Buckwheat A good summer crop but it comes to maturity in July/August so there is seldom room for it.

Perennial crops:
   Comfrey This is a very prolific producer of excellent compost material. The roots of one plant can be split up into numerous pieces and every one will grow. It needs to be kept free of weeds, though, and of course it needs a patch to itself. For that reason it is not a very practical crop for a small garden unless there is an out-of-the-way spot that you can spare or that is unsuitable for vegetables.
   Nettles Also make an excellent compost material and if regularly cut for this will remain under control. Raymond Bush, the writer on fruit-growing, recommended feeding nettles with sulphate of ammonia fertilizer to increase the amount of material for his compost heap. This might be a good idea for people who are desperately short of organic matter. The same could be done with comfrey.

There are several other green-manure crops, including the nitrogen-fixing lupins and clovers. The Henry Doubleday Research Association stocks a number of these and so do Chase Compost Seeds.

If we look at our plan, Figure 14 (see page 52) we can now get some idea of where green manure crops can be fitted in. Obviously a winter crop could follow broad and runner beans in rows 2a and 3a, and here they could in part be sown comparatively early (the broad beans and half the runner beans may both be finished by mid-August). Also, if, as suggested on page 57, these two crops are succeeded in the following year by purple sprouting broccoli and kale, the green manure can be allowed to grow on till the end of May by which time it will be producing an immense amount of foliage — but, of course, in this case it would have occupied space that could have grown edible crops.

Then, of course, from autumn onwards you will have started lifting your winter vegetables — for example, leeks, carrots, parsnips, swedes, turnips and beetroot, and in some cases you may have lifted the whole crop to store it. By November quite large spaces will have begun to appear all over the garden and these you can fill with winter beans. It would be wise at this point to consult your next year's plan to see how early you will be needing the ground next spring as it is really only worth while sowing green manure if the ground is not needed for crops before mid-April. But you may not yet have planned for next spring and, anyway, you may prefer to sow the green manure and leave it until you find you actually need the ground. Even if you have to clear the green manure in March when it has made very little growth it will nevertheless have made some, and it will have helped to conserve the soil from leaching, and to keep down the weeds.

It is more difficult to fit crops in in the summer when there is a lot of pressure on space. But most of your maincrop brassicas will be planted out after mid-June: this does not leave much time for growing a catch-crop before you plant them – except radishes, and there is a limit to the number of radishes a family can be expected to consume. So here would be a chance to fit in a quick crop of mustard. Then, although you will be intercropping between most of your fertile rows with summer vegetables, there will be some where this is not practicable. For example, there will not be space on either side of your climbing beans and maincrop peas to grow an edible inter-crop, and this is a good place to grow fenugreek which you can just use as a carpet to walk on when you want access for picking your beans, etc.

The golden rule is that, as well as producing crops for you, your garden is a natural phenomenon designed to perpetuate its own fertility by using sunlight to provide, through its leaves, the energy to convert simple chemicals into complex organic compounds and you must do all you can to allow, indeed, to encourage it to perform this vital function. To do this, you must strike a balance between keeping every available inch of ground carpeted with green leaf, and at the same time allowing your own edible crops ample space to grow without overcrowding.

There are three ways of using green manure crops. First, you can invert the soil and turn the crop in. But if there is any quantity of growth you will find that it is really difficult to restore the surface of the soil to a level and stable state that is suitable as a bed for the succeeding crop. Also, as the green manure crop decomposes and compacts, the soil above is going to subside and disturb the roots of the plants growing in it. The second alternative is to lift the whole crop and put it on the compost heap. This is the most straightforward of the three options, but it is important to realize that although you are in the long run increasing the fertility of your garden overall (because the decomposed green manure will eventually recycle as compost as much as or, if it is a legume, more nutrient than it took out in growing) you will be temporarily reducing the fertility of the soil where the crop grew, and this should be restored for the benefit of the crop to follow. The third method, which is mainly valuable for the legumes which fix nitrogen in their roots, is to hoe the crop off at ground level, put the green foliage on the compost heap, and leave the roots in the ground. The best way to do this is to use a billhook or shears to cut the green manure down to a few inches above soil level, and then use a finely sharpened hoe to complete the job. Ground which has grown a green-manure crop is usually free of weeds and, raked clean, will then be ready for the sowing of the next crop. Meanwhile, the green manure roots, with the nitrogen nodules, will rot down, releasing a slow steady flow of nitrogen for the following crop and providing a network of drainage channels in the topsoil, particularly valuable if you have a clay or fine silt soil.

If you find yourself really short of organic material, or if you are just taking over an infertile garden and wish to devote some time and space to building up its fertility you may decide to sacrifice some growing area entirely to growing green manure crops for a season or two. In this case it would be valuable, as well as concentrating on the nitrogen-fixing legumes, to give priority to some of the deep-rooting crops which will reach down to the subsoil and bring up some of the valuable nutrients that it contains.

Fodder radish and agricultural chicory are two deep-rooting annuals which combine well together and which also combine with annual lupin, a nitrogen fixer. If you are concentrating on rejuvenating a fairly large area, you may find it an advantage to turn your green manure crops in. You can then follow one crop immediately with a second one which will build on the first. For example, you could follow a summer crop of chicory with an autumn-sown one of tares which you hoe off next spring, leaving the roots in the soil. This would provide a good base for summer crops sown or planted out next June.

CHAPTER 8
SAVING SEED

Almost everyone has lurking in their potting shed or greenhouse an old squashed box of opened undated packets of seeds in addition to all sorts of loose unidentifiable seeds of unknown origin. The lettering on these packets is faded, the paper crinkled with ancient dampness, and although some are still almost full, most of them are not stored with sufficient care to ensure germination or to be any use. Some people also have an array of other boxes and containers with heads of leeks (or are they onions?) and parsnips, and dried-up pods of peas and beans all in a jumble; and, of course, tins full of runner bean seeds of unknown age and origin. Here again is a fruitful area for planning and creating order where a little trouble brings worthwhile rewards.

Seed is expensive, sometimes extortionate (fifteen seeds of salsify from a well-known seed-house cost me 35p in 1982). To grow a good range of vegetables one needs perhaps 30–50 packets in a season, costing from £15. 00 to £20. 00 (1986), or more if you go in for fancy F_1 hybrids. So, first of all you save money – I was still using in 1984 packets of sprouts, winter cauliflower and sprouting broccoli I bought from Chases in 1980, having saved myself nearly £30. 00 over that period. But it also enables you to be more adventurous because if you know your seeds are going to last you several years you are encouraged to buy several

varieties; for example, the winter cauliflowers I bought in 1980 consisted of five varieties which come to fruition at different times of the year, which I certainly would not have considered if it had involved buying five packets of seed every year for one vegetable.

A few seeds will not keep and are therefore not worth saving beyond the year in which they are bought, notably parsnip and scorzonera. The following seeds may be kept for the time stated – that is the number of years beyond the year they are designated for use.

1 year: pea, bean, salsify, parsley, summer and winter spinach, turnip and swede

2 years: tomato, leek

3 years: onion, spinach beet, seakale beet

4 years: lettuce, carrot

3–5 years: all brassicas except turnip and swede

6–7 years: marrow, courgette, cucumber, celeriac, celery

When finished with for the season, the seed packet should be folded over twice and secured with sealing tape or a paper clip. Make sure the packet is marked and dated. Sometimes the seed-merchant's information is printed right at the top of the packet and this is just the bit you cut off when opening it. It is a good plan to store these packets in tins; if you buy dried milk powder in tins with plastic lids they will do very well. Leave a teaspoonful or so of dried powder in the tins and this will absorb any moisture that gets in. Perhaps once or twice through the winter (especially if it is a very damp one) empty out the dried milk and replace it with a teaspoon or two of dry powder. In the autumn store the tins in a cool dry place until the following spring.

At all times try to avoid leaving packets of seed lying about in the greenhouse or on the kitchen window-sill where they may get very hot or, on occasions, wet.

If there is any doubt about the germination of old seeds, test a few of them. Get a small container (e.g., a plastic margarine tub with a lid), fold three or four layers of wet blotting paper or newspaper in it, shake a few seeds on to the wet paper, close the lid and place the tub in a reasonably warm place and check their germination over a reasonable period.

Another method of economizing on seeds is to save seed from plants in your garden. For some plants it is very worthwhile; for some it does not work at all; for some it is hardly worth it even though it works; and for a few (such as celery) the presence of seeding plants which bridge the gap between last season's plants and next can act as a host to pests. Another problem is that leaving a plant *in situ* after the rest of the crop has been cleared can interfere with your next crop's plans – it is really annoying, for example, to find the remains of a row of broad beans just where you want to plant out next season's cabbages. However, there is a way of overcoming this: many plants are quite attractive in flower and it is worth having a plant or two in the flower border or in the herb garden. The flowers of salsify and scorzonera do not make a great show but the seed-heads are the most beautiful gossamer

spheres shimmering in the evening sun – but even a light shower will annihilate them, so be sure to pick some on a fine summer day as soon as they mature. I usually sow half a dozen seeds in the flower bed and leave the best of the plants to go on to seed. You may prefer to select two of the best roots when you are lifting them, and transplant these two into the flower garden.

Opinions may differ about parsnip flowers – they are a handsome crown of yellow without a doubt, but some find them rather coarse for a flower border. If you do not like them very much, only one head needs to be left to seed as they produce an abundance of seeds. The same method can be used for onions and leeks, neither of which is out of place in the flower border. It is advisable to mark the plants as it is none too easy to distinguish them from each other at the seeding stage.

Sweet corn, marrow, courgette and tomato present few problems unless they are F_1 hybrids. It is no good keeping the seed of any F_1 hybrids because they do not breed true. Nor can any of the brassicas (cabbage, sprouts, cauliflowers, etc.) be kept usefully because they cross-pollinate – how lucky that these are the ones that last for several years so that buying them is not quite such an expense. Similarly, if you grow two or more varieties of peas or beans which flower simultaneously, grow them far apart (or at any rate grow the ones you need for seed far apart) because they too will cross-pollinate and the dominant one will oust the recessive one. If you use peas or beans in the row to produce seed it is worthwhile to mark off a number of plants at the end of the row and refrain from picking from these plants for eating. When you decide that you have enough pods for seed, pick off all new flowers and any small pods forming, so that the plant will direct all its energy to producing seed from the pods you have left. When you eventually need to clear the row lift the whole plant with a ball of soil on the roots and leave it to dry in the greenhouse or shed.

At the beginning of the season I take the seed packets out of their tins and arrange them in boxes – I am lucky enough to have acquired some excellent filing boxes about 6 inches (15cm) wide and 20 inches (50cm) long and these are ideal. I divide them off with cards into sections marked March/mid-April/end-April/mid-May/end-May/June/July/August, and put the seed packets in the appropriate section. As the seed is sown I remove the packet and as soon as the seedlings have appeared and I am sure I shall not need the packet again I throw the seed away (if its useful life is finished) or return it to its tin for next year, or if, like lettuces for example, it is to be sown successively, I advance it to the section when it should next be sown. I have boxes for the packets of smaller seeds and a separate one for large-seeded crops (peas, beans, etc.).

In this way I make sure that no crop is missed or overlooked, and I can easily tell what is due to be sown at any time – or all too often, what is overdue.

By these simple methods you can probably save up to three-quarters of your seed bill, and at the same time ensure that you can afford to maintain a wide range of all the varieties you do want to buy without breaking the bank.

There is some useful information about seeds and storage in Chapter 2 of *Know and Grow Vegetables (1)*, and Lawrence Hills has written a very good booklet on the subject called *Save Your Own Seed*, available from the HDRA.

CHAPTER 9
CROP ROTATION – THE PROS AND CONS

So now we come to crop rotation and to start with we must address the question: How important is it to rotate crops? How necessary? Opinions differ about this but I think in practice few gardeners do actually adhere to a strict rotation and not many to a rotation of any kind. My opinion is based partly on the fact that although most gardening experts pay lip-service to the need for rotation, none of them think it worth-while to devote very serious attention to it; but it is based mainly on observation. I am an insatiably curious peerer over hedges and through cracks in fences, and it is seldom that I see a garden that appears to be planned for a three or four year rotation. I think this is another of those time-honoured assumptions that are in need of re-assessment, so I shall put on the mantle of a sceptic and look at the whys and wherefores in a critical frame of mind. There are three principal reasons given in support of rotation:

(a) different crops require different nutrients and different soil conditions; if the same crop is grown year after year the soil will tend to become unbalanced and deficient in some respects, and may suffer what is known as 'soil sickness';

(b) many pests and diseases are specific to some crops or groups of crops and those that are soil-borne will build up over the years if the same crops continue to be grown on the same land;

(c) various processes in the management of the soil (e.g., manuring and liming) are best carried out when growing certain crops. Without a rotation of crops and, thus, of these accompanying operations they will be carried out haphazardly and it will be difficult to keep a check on them so as to ensure that the whole of the garden is regularly treated.

Let us now look at each of these reasons in support of rotation in more detail:

(a) *Nutrients and soil conditions*
The sort of effect referred to here is that, for example, beans are greedy for potash and so if you continue to grow them in the same spot your soil will eventually suffer from potash deficiency. The short answer is this: No it won't! Not if you fertilize it properly, preferably with compost or composted manure. And the second answer is: If it does, make good the deficiency! What could be simpler? Apply potash fertilizer or wood ash or Russian comfrey, and in the future take more care of your fertilizing programme. But then it is also said that in general it is far better to vary the crops by rotation so as to maintain a balance of demand which is met by a balance of natural fertilizers than it is to upset the balance by continually growing the same crop and then having to make good the deficiencies in a piecemeal fashion.

Well, I think there is something to this, but if we are looking to nature to guide us, this latter is exactly what nature does do: wild plants do tend to grow year after year in clumps in the same place where conditions happen to suit them best, and in spite of this they do not seem to create any soil deficiencies, or if they do, the deficiencies do not seem to prevent them thriving. For example, hedgerows contain a wide variety of plants along their length but how often are we struck by a proud array of foxgloves for quite some distance after which there is not another foxglove for miles. Or the far corner of a field where the sprays do not reach and the ground has a waterlogged slope down to a ditch, will startle you with a blaze of marsh marigolds which, herbicides permitting, will remain in the same spot for decades. Your garden, too, may have similar variations, one part naturally more fertile, another silty and hard, another inclined to acidity, and it is possible that in our enthusiasm for achieving a uniform consistency we are destroying the advantages that a natural variation offers. Unfortunately, because so little research has been done into natural ways of gardening (naturally, because it carries no profit for those who pay for research) we do not really know the answer to this, and so we assume without thinking that it is best to aim for an overall balanced uniformity.

Another type of argument of a similar nature is often made. To give an example, it runs roughly as follows: potatoes are averse to lime, so if you grow potatoes on the same soil year after year you will never have a chance to lime it and it will become more and more acid. Again, I say: if potatoes prefer an acid soil why is there any need to lime it, so long as one continues to grow potatoes there? Indeed, it seems to me that the opposite may be the case, for where rotation results in the whole garden being limed on a regular basis there will be insufficient variation throughout the garden to accommodate the different needs of plants. Suppose you find your garden shows the first signs of club-root. Then one immediate countermeasure will be to lime your brassica patch substantially down to a depth of at least 6 inches (15cm). Your brassicas may be followed next year or the year after by potatoes and although you may well not lime it again there will still be substantial residues of lime remaining on the potato plot, especially if you follow the advice generally given to use ground limestone rather than hydrated lime. However, I do not wish to be misleading about potatoes, and there are other and better reasons for rotating your potato crop which will be dealt with below.

Another reason often given, is that if you grow the same crop year after year a condition known as soil-sickness develops which is very difficut to remedy. I have thought about this and I admit there have been occasions when I have looked at some crop that has succumbed to disease or disaster and I have felt defensively: 'It's not my fault, it's nothing to do with me! It must be soil-sickness'. But the trouble is that soil-sickness is so difficult to recognize or identify, because the people who write or talk about it do not seem to have any idea what it is. It is all rather vague, and I suggest that to be accurate soil-sickness is not in itself a condition, but that it describes a symptom (poor growth) for which no explanation has been discovered – in other words, for which you have not managed to identify the cause. It may be due to a decline in nutrition, it may be due to a build-up of disease, it may be some other, as yet unknown, factor. I suspect that it may often result from mis-management – see the example of the Cornish broccoli growers mentioned on page 97.

You may think I am merely setting up Aunt Sallies for the fun of knocking them down again. No, I do have genuine worries about growing the same crops year after year and I can see the point of rotation in theory: my doubts centre on its effectiveness in practice. It involves limitations of what you can grow and considerable rigidity in your planning and I am far from convinced about the wisdom of plunging into a strict rotation unless you have pressing reasons to do so. However, there are more powerful reasons in its favour than those we have been considering so far, to which we must now turn our attention.

(b) *Pests and diseases*
The most important reason for rotating crops is the build-up of pests and diseases in the soil. This particularly applies to eelworm in potatoes and tomatoes and club-root in brassicas, but it also applies to a lesser extent to other crops which suffer from pests and diseases that over-winter in the soil; for example, beans (anthracnose, root rot) and onions (eelworm and several fungus diseases, such as whiterot).

There is no cure for potato eelworm but there are some potato varieties that are resistant to most, but not all, eelworms (there are many different varieties of eelworm). Their eggs are contained in cysts, each of which contains 2–400 eggs and which lie dormant in the soil for up to six or seven years. Each year some of the eggs hatch and if there is no crop to feed off they die, so that in seven years or so the ground will be cleared. The presence of a suitable crop is signalled by excretions from the roots and this causes a greatly increased rate of eelworm hatching; the resultant larvae then feed off the plant roots and give rise to a further much more numerous batch of cysts. Early varieties tend to suffer more than maincrops, which makes the immunity of the Cornish early potato-growers (see page 97) even more significant. If your soil is very badly infested you may have to avoid growing potatoes (and tomatoes) for seven or eight years, but a three or four year rotation, combined with growing eelworm-resistant varieties should keep it comparatively immune (see page 141 for a way of combining a six-year rotation for potatoes with a three-year one for other crops). But you must be careful when lifting the crop to remove all potatoes as any remaining to grow as a weed the following or subsequent years will, of course, act as host to the pest and nullify your efforts.

Club-root is a fungus which can live in the soil for nine years or more. There is no cure but some degree of prevention is obtained by heavy application of lime which, if possible, should be worked into the top 6 inches (15cm) of the soil. There are no immune varieties, but cauliflowers and cabbages are the most susceptible crops. Unfortunately, there are a number of weeds belonging to the cruciferae family which are also susceptible to club-root (and therefore, of course, hosts to its continued propagation in the soil). So, unless you can keep your garden free from these various weeds (which include shepherds purse, charlock and wild radish), it is not possible to eliminate completely the risk of club-root. And even then, there is the risk that some neighbourly fellow from a nearby allotment will make you an unsolicited gift of several clods of contaminated soil from his wellingtons as he comes to pass the time of day.

When I was young it was believed by some parents that it would benefit children to be brought up in a sort of antiseptic disease-free shangri-la, and several families attempted to achieve this with the help of air filters, sterilization, copious antiseptics and other technological marvels. Unfortunately, as well as producing several varieties of child neurosis never before encountered, it was found that as soon as the resulting adults were exposed in the wider world to infectious diseases which they had not previously encountered and, therefore, not built up any resistance to, they had no defences and succumbed to them like nine-pins. Similarly, you can never isolate your crops entirely from attack. There is no wide-ranging formula that guarantees immunity. New ideas of cultivation (no-digging, raised beds, etc.) are dredged up continually, promising unprecedented success. Old ideas (deep trenching, mulching) are revived. I think this questioning and questing attitude is all to the good and has brought undoubted benefits – but no sure-fire solution to the problem of trouble-free gardening. Similarly, we have a constant outpouring of new pesticides and fungicides, but many people – not just the growing organic movement – are worried at their possible long-term effects and are reluctant to use them. In addition, they are costly, their use is time-consuming, they require skill and experience for success, and they do not always live up to expectations.

Rotation is only one amongst many measures we can take, and is valuable in combination with other forms of prevention. There are occasions that call particularly for its use, the most important being the first attack by soil-borne diseases such as club-root, eelworm, white rot, etc. Early signs of club-root, for example, should alert you to a whole range of counter-action: infected plants should be removed immediately and burned; the garden's acidity should be measured and lime applied to a depth of 6–8 inches (15–20cm); drainage should be checked and, if necessary, improved. You should trace where the infected plants came from, and, if from a shop or supplier, you may feel it worth going and having it out with them; in any case take note never to buy from that source again, and if possible to grow your own plants in future. If the plants came from your own seed-bed, regard that as infected land, and do not use it for brassicas again. For next season select an area as far as possible from any brassicas you are growing this year. Feed the garden with extra organic fertilizer and compost – and so on. Then, too, there are methods by which you may still obtain a crop from infected land, and there is the possibility of sterilizing your soil – all these will be found in the gardening books listed on page 153; these methods are no part of planning and are not covered in this book. And finally, of course, nine-tenths of the battle is to grow healthy crops that are sturdy enough to resist attack or to flourish even when under attack.

(c) *Management of the soil*
The third reason for rotation is that along with the rotation of crops goes a rotation of operations; for example, as referred to earlier, liming. There is a traditional routine for these: manure the peas, beans and onions, add lime to the brassicas, add fertilizers for potatoes and roots, thus ensuring that all the land is treated equally over a three-year period.

If planting proceeds haphazardly so also will these operations, and it will be quite difficult to keep a check on them to make sure that all the garden is treated regularly. Undoubtedly, rotation is a convenience from this point of view

Intercropping Little Gem lettuces with Musselburgh leeks. Using the space between your rows ensures maximum productivity if you plan it carefully.

Japanese onions. The sets can be sown as late as October to be harvested the following June or early July.

Lamb's lettuce is a vegetable to grow if you want to try something
a bit different – very nice in salads.

The variety of cabbages is enormous, but this one, the Ormskirk, is
a good late cabbage.

– but it is no more than that and I do not think this adds substantially to the arguments in favour of rotation: it is not really so difficult to keep a check on it in other ways.

We now come to another consideration: is effective rotation *possible* in a small garden? I have already mentioned the problem of related weeds, such as shepherd's purse hosting club-root. There are similar problems with hedgerow plants; for example, wild carrot and other umbelliferous plants host carrot root fly; and Jerusalem artichokes (usually regarded as the most innocent and trouble-free crop) carry lettuce root aphid. In fact, there are very few pests or diseases which are so specific that there is not some other plant or common weed or wild flower which is susceptible to it and therefore hosts it. But the biggest difficulty is that most gardens are very limited in size, gardeners are continually moving from one crop to another and as they do so they carry soil on their boots and on their garden tools and it is this soil which spreads the pest. Although you can take great care to burn all infected plant remains, it is far from easy to achieve this. Some umbelliferous weeds will grow, some potatoes will remain unobserved, some eelworm cysts will fall off the plant and remain in the soil, and so on.

For these and similar reasons many people believe that rotation is a waste of time because you cannot isolate each section of your garden from the others as farmers operating on a field scale can isolate their fields, and because some pests (such as white rot) are so persistent that once you have them no rotation will ever get rid of them.

What is indisputable is that there is a minimum practicable size of garden for a proper rotation. I feel that the half allotment we considered in Chapter 4 is below that limit. Each of its four plots are 4.5 × 4.5m (15 feet by 15 feet) which gives six 4.5m rows, a total row-length of 27m (30 yards). This is just too small, too cramped, with each plot so closely surrounded by its neighbours for a rotation to be effective. I speak from experience because although I have quite a good-sized garden, I do actually grow most of my vegetables on a half-allotment of this size. I do practise a sort of rough and ready rotation for onion crops (no main-crop onions, though), potatoes (two rows only), and brassicas (nearly half the allotment, but some of them are transferred to the garden). I would not be happy with a strict rotation; I would find it too limiting and so far I have not believed it necessary. Instead I am building up the soil's fertility and health with deep cultivation and massive applications of compost and seaweed. I have not been here long enough to claim that I have yet got it disease-free, or think that I ever will do. I belong to that group of people who believe that the best thing to do is to grow plants really well, using resistant varieties wherever possible, using organic manures and composts, and avoiding powerful pesticides which upset the natural balance and destroy the predators (such as ladybirds, centipedes and stag beetles) which feed on pests and exercise some control over them, and your crops will be sturdy enough to survive all but the worst attacks. We instance the case of Cornish farmers who used to manure their land with seaweed which they gathered from Mounts Bay and built into enormous compost heaps with crop residues, hedge trimmings and every bit of organic matter they could lay their hands on. For a hundred and fifty years or more they grew a continuous succession of new potatoes and winter cauliflowers (in those pre-EEC days known as Cornish broccoli) on the same fields year in and year out without suffering attacks of either potato eel-worm or club-root or cabbage root fly. During the last thirty years they have pretty well all abandoned this manuring programme in favour of chemical ferti-lizers because of the high cost of labour and for the first time they are beginning to suffer from club-root as well as other troubles such as short-stemmed ane-mones.

I do strongly believe that well-grown plants in well-composted soil stand a better chance of survival and (whatever the chemists may say) produce healthier and more nutritious crops. However, I am not one of those over-optimistic people who think that a barrowload of compost will ensure instant success and a guarantee of immunity from all pests and diseases. After all, if we have a preference for compost-grown broad beans, what are the grounds for de-nying blackfly a similar preference? I have never noticed that the pigeons favour my neighbour's chemically ferti-lized allotment rather than mine, and I do not see why lesser creatures should do so either.

However, to come back to rotation – what is the answer? How do you decide? To be sure, most writers and 'experts' do recommend rotation, but they tend to do so with an off-hand nonchalance that is hard to take serious-ly. They imply that it is something you decide to do and hey presto you do it: no problems, no sweat; and if you do have problems, never mind, 'it may be expedient to break the rules' to quote Allan Jackson in his excellent *Observer's Book of Vegetables*. Obviously this is a very difficult choice and there is no definitive answer to it. It is to some extent a matter which depends not just on balancing up the pros and cons but on your feelings

about them, so let us just summarize the pros and cons again briefly.

Pro: It certainly helps you to keep free from disease, though it offers no guarantee of this. It is probably essential if there are signs that your garden is seriously prone to some diseases such as club-root or already infested with them. It helps to ensure that the various garden tasks are carried out systemati-cally and regularly. It can, once you get into the routine of it, ensure a very orderly system of gardening.

Con: It does to quite an extent limit the choice of crops that you can grow; a four-year rotation limits it considerably. It is inflexible because once you have decided on a plan it is not easy to change your mind or find space for plants you have been given at the last minute, and so on. It requires careful planning in advance, preferably over several years.

Perhaps in the end the decision will depend on your temperament and your approach to life generally. If you are a very orderly well-organized person, rotation will be well within your compass, and will be a challenge that will give you a lot of satisfaction to meet. If you are – how shall I put it? – a 'spontaneous' gardener you may find it an anxiety and a straitjacket that will take too much of the pleasure out of gardening. Do not ever forget that economically the average good allot-ment gardener is earning the equivalent of 40p per hour or thereabouts (heaven knows what the average bad one is totting up), so economically you would do far better to go out as a jobbing gardener and earn an untaxed two or three pounds an hour on the black economy and buy your vegetables in the local market. But then for gardeners it is not the balance sheet that matters so much, it is the joy of having your own patch of soil on which you can grow your own fine fresh uncontaminated produce in your own style that counts. Growing food, making the best use of the land of which we are the stewards and for which we are responsible to this and future generations, is indeed a serious matter and must be taken seriously. On the other hand it must not become a burden. Plants depend on how you treat them, and thus they respond to your mood. It may sound fey to claim that a joyful attitude will produce monster cauliflowers – but I often wonder: how many depressives and pessimists have green fingers?

If you are still uncertain about this decision, obviously the first thing to do is to read the chapters on rotation to see what is involved, before you choose.

CHAPTER 10
PLANS AND DIAGRAMS

Before we come to work out an actual rotation, there is one more matter to be disposed of, or, I should say, clarified.

Up until now I have tried to avoid bringing in complicated plans and diagrams because I know that many people have a mental barrier against them (I do myself as a matter of fact). But when it came to planning in Chapter 4 they could not be avoided easily. However, at that stage we used both plans and diagrams on a bit of an *ad hoc* basis without clearly establishing the differences between them. But when it comes to rotations it is more important to be clear about this distinction. They often look alike and indeed often are alike, but there is a fundamental difference between them. A plan is a representation or map of something. It may emphasize some particular characteristic, as a street plan of a big city gives special prominence to the streets, but basically it is a scaled-down simplified picture or map. A diagram, on the other hand, is a convenient way of presenting visually any information you are specially interested in so that it is easy to understand. If you know London you will be familiar with what is known as the 'Plan of the Underground', but this is misnamed. Strictly speaking it is not a plan, it is a diagram that shows you which lines to take for a particular destination, and where to change, but it does not show you, as a plan would, the

actual course and direction of the lines.

Analytical readers will realize that a plan is actually a particular sort of diagram – it is a diagram designed to show a scaled-down simplified representation of something, usually as it is seen from above. But other diagrams show different aspects; for example, how something changes with time, or how to use something. So it is important when you see what looks like a diagram or a plan to be clear what it aims to show – and just as important what it does not aim to show.

So now we are going to draw a diagram of a garden, and this will not be designed to show a plan of it, but to provide a convenient format for listing the plots and rows over successive years as a basis for working out a three- or four-year rotation. For the moment we are concentrating on a four-year rotation; first, let us take the simple case of an allotment or a rectangular garden. Figure 20 shows a picture of it, drawn in June.

And Figure 21 shows a plan, derived from the picture.

What the picture does not bring out is that this garden is divided into four plots, which are, in fact, being cropped in a way suitable for a four-year rotation, but this will be made clear by developing the plan. I shall leave out the bit at the right-hand end with the

Figure 20: An allotment

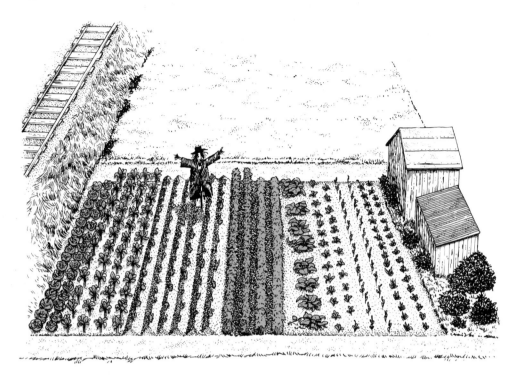

Figure 21: Plan of the allotment above showing the basic four-year rotation plots

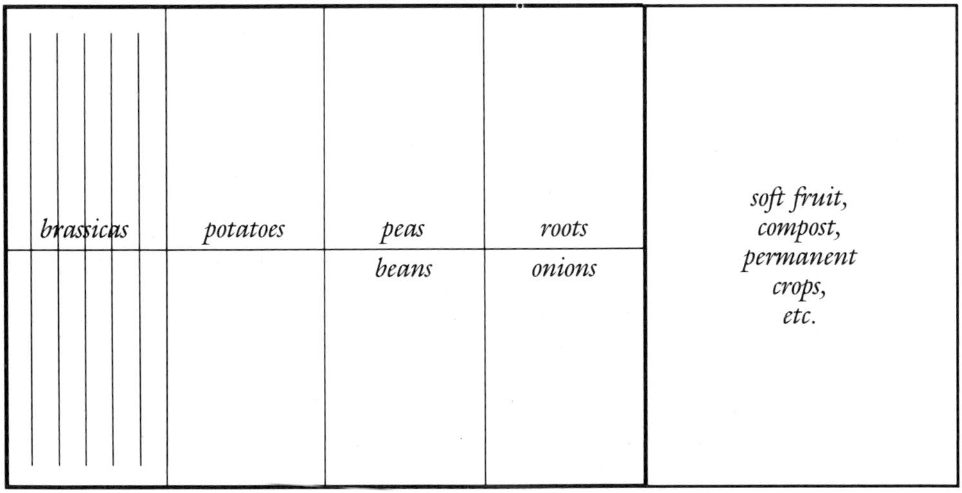

brassicas	potatoes	peas beans	roots onions	soft fruit, compost, permanent crops, etc.

compost heap, shed, soft fruit, etc. and concentrate on the vegetable patch. We are already familiar with this plan because it is similar to the one in Chapter 4 for a half-allotment.

Let us now draw a diagram of each of these plots over one season. Again, this is similar to what we did in Figure 12 in Chapter 4. We marked in the months (excluding the dormant winter months) horizontally and the rows vertically. We then marked in each square the state of that row in each month. So, for example, we might plant onions in row 1 in March and we would mark it in as in Figure 22. In April the crop is still

Figure 22: Crop planted

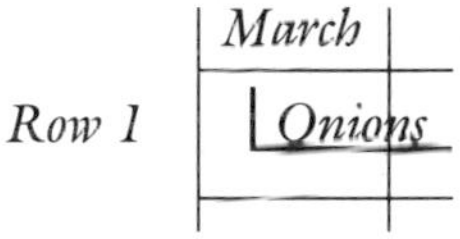

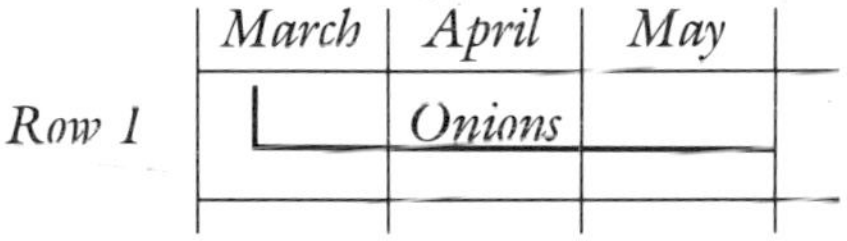

growing, so we mark it in as in Figure 23. And in May it is still growing (see Figure 24). Now in this last figure it is beginning to look as if we are drawing a plan of our row 1, the bar being a simplified representation of the row of onions. This is not so. The thick horizontal line indicates that during the month under which it appears (March, April, May, in this case) Row 1 has a crop on it (whereas a thin unmarked horizontal line indicates that there is no crop growing there). This information

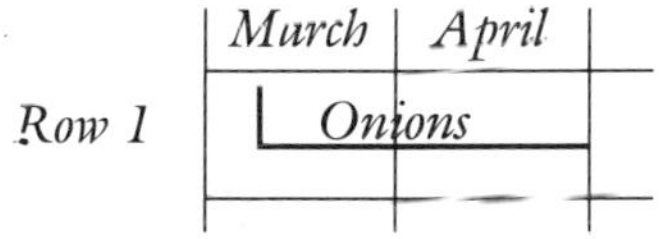

could equally well have been conveyed by ticks as in Figure 25.

Figure 25: An alternative method of marking using ticks

	March	April	May
		Onions	
Row 1	✔	✔	✔

Perhaps this would have been less confusing but, as we shall see later, not so convenient for providing information – for example it is not very easy to show clearly which part of the month the crop was planted and harvested. So our completed diagram providing information about Row 1 over the season is shown as in Figure 26.

This shows that an onion crop was (or will be) grown there, planted in mid-March and harvested in mid-August. In a similar way we can now complete our diagram for plot 1, which is shown in Figure 27, before any crops have been indicated on it.

Note that I have done the same as I did in Chapter 4 – I have divided each row into two, so that row 1 is marked as row 1a and row 1b, each 15 feet (4.5m) long. If we now draw four of these plots and put them alongside each other we have a diagram of the complete allotment. Note that in the picture (Figure 20) the rows run across the allotment from edge to edge, as they do also in the plan (Figure 21), whereas in the diagram (Figure 28) the lines run from end to end of the allotment. If you think I must have got this wrong, or if it puzzles you, you have not quite understood the distinction between plans and diagrams and I suggest you read again from the beginning of this chapter, bearing Figure 28 in mind.

In Figure 9 we showed rows 1 and 2. This gave a bit more information still: it showed roughly the size the plants in the row had reached at any particular

Figure 26: Complete diagram showing crop over a season

	March	April	May	June	July	Aug	Sept	Oct	Nov
Row 1			Onions						

date. This might sometimes be useful, by indicating at a glance whether there is room between the rows for intercropping. The only trouble with this is that unless it is done fairly accurately it can be misleading – and it is not easy to draw it in accurately. One is tempted to do it roughly by guesswork and, in fact, if you look at my diagram you will be struck by how smoothly the curves of the crops in rows 1 and 2 glide gracefully down to make space for the increasing curve of the intercropping row. That is artistic licence – it has no basis in fact because I do not even state what these crops are going to be, and, of course, it could be seriously misleading. This is one of the dangers of too much careful planning and too many predic-

tions. Gardening is by its nature unpredictable and it is not helpful to have a diagram which appears to give at a glance a precise indication of how much space there is between crops when in actual fact it is based on guesswork or on a rough estimate. It is more useful for the diagram to match our imprecision so that we do not get a false impression, and so that when we use it we will allow some leeway.

Also, of course, we are making a diagram of twenty-four rows and probably as many inter-rows and to mark each one in this way could be quite time-consuming and probably look rather messy if you have to make a number of changes. So, generally, I find it better to work with a very simple line to

Figure 27: Diagram of Plot 1 over one season

PLOT 1 – Brassicas

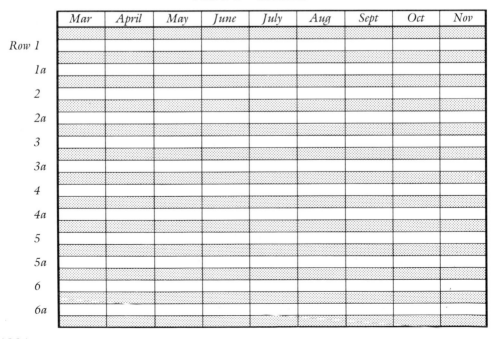

	Mar	April	May	June	July	Aug	Sept	Oct	Nov
Row 1									
1a									
2									
2a									
3									
3a									
4									
4a									
5									
5a									
6									
6a									

Figure 28: Diagram of whole allotment over one season

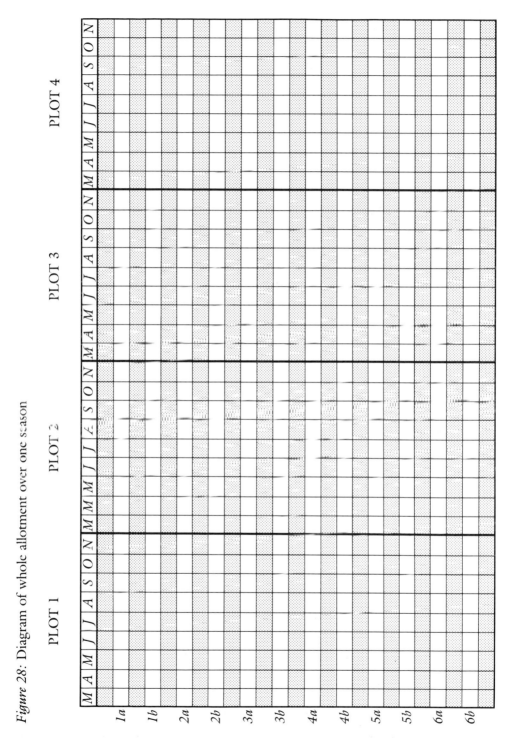

Figure 29:   222 Acacia Grove

indicate when I expect to plant or to work with a very simple line to indicate when I expect to plant or sow and when I expect to lift crops, with dots to indicate when it is spread over a period, and with dots and a line when the precise date of harvesting is especially uncertain.

So we now have a picture of your allotment, a plan of your allotment, and a blank diagram of your allotment which later we will be using to plan your rotation and to fill in with winter crops and intercrops. Many vegetable gardens are like this – rectangular with rows going straight across or along, and in such cases the diagram and the plan will look, as here, very similar. But, if your garden is not like this, but is all curves and curls, it is still possible to

represent it on a simple diagram of this sort. So let us take another example, a little less straightforward. Figure 29 shows a picture of no 222 Acacia Grove, whose owners are of an artistic, imaginative turn of mind.

Ignoring Venus and the fleshy dolphins etc., we shall draw a simple plan (Figure 30). We now have to divide this into four roughly equal areas, each of which will be one plot in the rotation. The best way to do this is to mark out the rows since, after all, it is they rather than the actual area that determine the effective size of each plot. In practice, if you follow the advice given in Chapter 4 you will be marking out your rows with permanent markers; this would be a good time to measure these up. Make each row the distance apart you have

Figure 30:   Plan of 222 Acacia Grove

decided on (in our caes 80cm) and for the moment put in a temporary marker (because we may find later that we want to change some rows). Measure each row's length and keep a record of this on the plan as shown. You will see that, due to the proximity of Venus, not all the rows go in the same direction, so we mark this fact on our plan. (I have marked the lengths in metres, but if you prefer imperial measurements, add nought and divide by three – so 1m = 10 divided by 3 = 3.3 feet.)

Now, add up the total length of your rows, which is 69m in the left-hand bed and 69.25m in the two right-hand beds, making 138m in all. For a rotation your plots should be as nearly equal in size as possible, so each plot will have roughtly a quarter of this total, that is, 34.5m of row. This means that the left-hand and right-hand sides are near enough equal to two plots each, but the top right-hand section is nowhere near large enough to be a plot on its own, so it will have to incorporate a chunk from the section below. So now we have four plots (Figure 31). Notice, by the way, that I have ignored the permanent crops for simplicity – perhaps we can imagine these being accommodated beyond the compost heap with soft fruit, etc.

It is convenient from the point of view of planning to have rows of equal length (though not absolutely essential). In practice this often cannot be done, but it is usually possible to achieve it in effect by combining or splitting rows. For example, Figure 32 shows two ways in which the top left-hand plot can be divided into six rows of roughly 5.5m each.

Now we can set about using these simplfied plans of your four plots to make four diagrams, which will then be combined to give a diagram of the

Figure 31: The four plots for 222 Acacia Grove

Figure 32:   Two ways of dividing the top plot

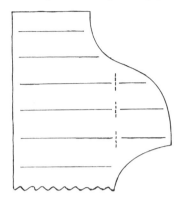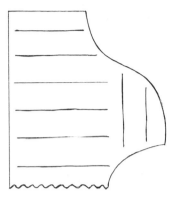

whole garden. All we do is to take each of the six rows and make a diagram across the page on which its progress throughout the season can be plotted from month to month, as we did in Figure 26. We then set the six rows beneath each other allowing space for the inter-rows between them. This gives us a diagram of the whole plot for one season. Finally, we join the diagrams of the four plots together into one. This will give us a rectangular diagram with the rows down the vertical side and the months of the growing season across the page.

So now we have our complete garden, in diagram form (Figure 33). If you look back to the diagram of the allotment in Figure 28 you will see that the diagram we have just completed is almost exactly the same. And that is as it should be – the same type of simple diagram can represent a garden of any shape; all you have to do is to make sure that the rows marked in the diagram correspond to actual rows in the garden, and that you have an accurate record of which these are. And, for that matter, it need not be of actual rows; it can be parts of rows, patches sown broadcast, raised beds, or mounds, or whatever you fancy. But, of course, if

you are following the system I am developing in this book, it will probably be rows.

There is another difference between Acacia Grove and our allotment besides its shape, and that is its size. Each of its plots has a total row length of 34.5m (113 feet) whereas in our allotment each plot has a length of 54m (177 feet). I think the former is very cramped for a proper rotation, though it might be attempted since the garden is already to some extent divided into plots.

So, now we have our diagram for one season and from this is devised the diagram for the whole rotation. To begin with we shall simplify it by leaving out the individual rows and treating each plot in a general way: that is, we shall mark plot 1 as the brassica plot without going into the details of which brassicas we grow and which row we grow them in. Also, to save space, I shall give each group a distinguishing letter as follows:

A Brassicas
B Potatoes, tomatoes
C Peas and beans (legumes)
D Roots, onions, etc.

This is just to simplify the diagram and economize on space. Do not worry

Figure 33: Diagram for 222 Acacia Grove

	PLOT 1									PLOT 2									PLOT 3								PLOT 4									
	M	*A*	*M*	*J*	*J*	*A*	*S*	*O*	*N*	*M*	*A*	*M*	*J*	*J*	*A*	*S*	*O*	*N*	*M*	*A*	*M*	*J*	*J*	*A*	*S*	*O*	*N*	*M*	*A*	*M*	*J*	*J*	*A*	*S*	*O*	*N*
Row 1																																				
2																																				
3																																				
4																																				
5																																				
6																																				

for the moment which crops the letters stand for. Now I shall start from the diagram of the allotment shown in Figure 28 (though the method is just the same if I start from the diagram of the garden in Acacia Grove) and I can represent that like this:

Plot 1	Plot 2	Plot 3	Plot 4
Crop A	Crop B	Crop C	Crop D

From now on I shall not use the letters A, B, C and D to stand for anything except the crops I have listed above, so there is no need to keep repeating the word 'crop'. Also, whenever I am using this diagram to represent the state of a garden at any time, I shall always put the plots in this same order 1, 2, 3, 4; so again there is no need to write it in, you can assume that this diagram

A	B	C	D

means the same as the diagram above. The only thing I have missed out so far is to indicate which year I am talking about, this year, next year, the year after next and so on. So I shall call this year Year 1, in which case a complete description of your garden as it is in the picture is shown on our diagram like this:

Year 1	A	B	C	D

and you know immediately that this means that this year crop A (brassicas) is being grown in plot 1, crop B in plot 2, and so on.

Well now, brassicas (crop A) are followed by potatoes (crop B), potatoes by legumes (crop C), legumes by onions (crop D) and onions by brassicas again, so, using our diagram, we can say that next year we will have:

Year 2	B	C	D	A

the following year;

Year 3	C	D	A	B

the year after that;

Year 4	D	A	B	C

and the year after that;

Year 5	A	B	C	D

which is, of course, the same as year 1 when we start the rotation again.

So a complete diagram of the four-year rotation is this:

Plot	1	2	3	4
Year 1	A	B	C	D
Year 2	B	C	D	A
Year 3	C	D	A	B
Year 4	D	A	B	C

which in fact can be written without confusion as:

A	B	C	D
B	C	D	A
C	D	A	B
D	A	B	C

Now the key to the rotation is the succession of crops which takes place in each plot, so what we are really concerned with is this succession:

A
B
C
D

but as this is quite awkward to write and wastes space, I shall write it like this:

A	B	C	D

and to distinguish it from the diagram

of your whole garden in year 1 which is written:

Year 1 | A | B | C | D |

I shall write it as:

Plot 1 | A | B | C | D |

I think it is obvious that the history of your garden over the rotation can be inferred from the history of one plot, or from the overall state of the garden in any one year. I should make it clear that we are, of course, not necessarily bound to grow exactly the same crops within each plot every year; in year 1 we can grow sprouts, swedes and sprouting broccoli in the brassica plot and in year 2 kale, cabbages and cauliflowers, and so on – what you can tell from this simplified diagram is which plot they must go in; since they are brassicas they must always go in the plot marked A. Referring back to the diagram of the four-year rotation, they will go in plot 1 in year 1, plot 4 in year 2, and so on. For most of the time it is the plot diagram you will use to plan the detailed rotation and from that you can easily read off the state of the garden at any time, what you should be sowing and planting and where it should go.

I hope all this has not seemed too onerous. These diagrams are not really complicated, but they may seem so at first sight. Once you have become familiar with them through use, they will all slot into place. Also, you may be cheered by the fact that if all goes well quite a lot of this will only have to be done once in a lifetime because, as I have explained, the rows will remain permanent, and the basic rotation can remain permanent too.

CHAPTER 11
FOUR-YEAR ROTATION – THE MAIN CROPS

The rotations usually recommended are the three-year rotation and the four-year rotation. Choosing between these two is a bit arbitrary because they are both compromises. To be completely immune from potato eelworm, a six-year rotation is necessary and from clubroot at least a nine-year one – and even then absolute immunity is impossible to achieve. It is, in fact, possible to have a six-year rotation for potatoes under certain circumstances (see page 141), but a nine-year rotation for brassicas would be so limiting that it would only be undertaken if your garden was infested with disease, in which case it would probably be better to give up growing brassicas altogether for a period.

A four-year rotation does impose a lot of constraints on your cropping plan; a three-year one is far more flexible. I think that a three-year rotation has the advantages and disadvantages set out in Chapter 9 to some extent and that a four-year rotation has them to a greater extent. There is, having said this, an unsatisfactory vagueness about the exact extent of the advantages and disadvantages of each rotation plan and, consequently, an unsatisfactory vagueness about which of these to practise.

The essence of a four-year rotation is that your garden is divided up into four, roughly equal plots and that the following groups of crops rotate round them

so that each group is only grown in any one plot once in four years:
Brassicas (cabbage, cauliflower, etc.)
Potato and tomato
Pea and bean
Root crops and the onion family

The important point to emphasize is not so much that, for example, brassicas must be grown in the first year in Plot 1, the next year in plot 2, the next in plot 3, and so on, but that they must *not* be grown in any plot except for the one allocated to them.

There are a number of crops which do not fall into any of these groups, such as artichokes, lettuce, chicory, saladings, sweet corn, marrow, courgette, spinach, spinach and seakale beet, celery and celeriac. Many of the arguments in favour of rotation apply equally to these crops, so that, if you decide that crop rotation is a worthwhile idea, you will probably want to rotate these as well. It does not matter which group you put them in but, having once allocated them, say, to the potato plot they should be grown in that plot throughout the rotation.

Some people may agree that rotation is a good idea, but will ask why this particular order (brassicas, then potato, then pea/bean, then onion/roots, then brassicas again, and so on) has been given when it is usually recommended that brassicas should follow pea/bean.

Many people grow brassicas after peas/beans because pea and bean plants fix nitrogen from the atmosphere and if the roots are left in the soil when the crop is lifted the nitrogen they contain will be released gradually and this will particularly benefit brassicas. This makes a lot of sense. The reason I do not choose this order is as follows: peas and beans are summer crops, so most of this plot will be cleared at the end of the summer and this provides an opportunity to grow several rows of green manure over the winter. Winter green manure crops are not very valuable unless they are allowed to grow on until late April or May. Although main winter brassicas are not planted out until well after this date, summer brassica crops (which can only be grown in this plot) need to be sown or planted early in the spring and this would be very difficult to fit in if the ground were occupied by green manures. If you do not propose to grow green manures and do not grow any other over-wintering crops, or if you do not want to grow summer cabbage, cauliflower, kohlrabi, etc., perhaps the pea/bean then brassica succession is the best.

I shall explain my preference for having brassicas follow the root crops. Root crops usually remain in the ground till late autumn or early winter. Except in the North of Britain many of them can be left after this until they are used. So the possibility of having a following crop of green manure is greatly reduced. On the other hand, root crops will not usually last beyond March, or if they do they can be lifted and stored, and thus make way for early summer brassicas to occupy the space.

There is, of course, nothing sacrosanct about the order I have chosen and I think that the precise order is not all that important, it is a matter of choosing whichever you find most convenient and this will depend partly on the crops you are proposing to grow. Let us consider the four plots and groups of crops in order:

1. *The brassica plot* The main winter brassicas – sprouts, broccoli, cauliflower – must have a firm soil to grow in (it is not so important for the other brassicas). Not just a firm topsoil either because the roots of brassicas do not grow in the topsoil, they grow mainly 6–8 inches (15–20cm) below it and extend downwards. So it is no good lifting previous crops, weeding and preparing the soil and then stamping it down on the surface a week or so before you plant out the brassicas. This will merely create a firm crust on top of a loose sub-soil, which is the opposite of what you want. I believe that it is the failure to plant brassicas firmly enough that is responsible for many of the difficulties and disappointments that people have with these crops.

It is, in fact, quite difficult to create a firm sub-soil straightaway by tamping or stamping it down, and so the best thing to do is to carry out any cultivation that is necessary, including the lifting of previous crops, a month or six weeks in advance, leave the soil to settle and then stamp it down. It is better, therefore, for brassicas to follow a crop that has been lifted at least four to six weeks before the brassicas are due for planting.

Even if you plant them out as late as the beginning of July (which you can do if you use the method set out on pages 64–66), the ground should be cleared fairly early in May.

2. *The potato/tomato plot* Some people grow their whole year's supply of potatoes, which will take up most of the plot. Others limit themselves to earlies. Also, people with greenhouses or walls that catch the sun, may grow their tomatoes there rather than in the

vegetable garden. So the potato/tomato plot is one that can leave a large or small amount of space for other crops.

If you do not intend to grow potatoes, you may find it quite difficult to fill this plot. You will, of course, be able to grow many more summer vegetables. For instance, you can grow more peas and beans on the pea/bean plot and move most of your other summer vegetables to the potato/tomato plot. Or it may be wiser for you to go for a three-year rotation, missing out the potato year altogether. This would enable you to grow more brassicas and winter roots, which would achieve a better balance between summer and winter crops.

It is rather unlikely that you will be attempting to grow aubergines or sweet peppers in the vegetable garden rather than in some special, sheltered, sunny spot, but, if you do, you should grow them in the potato plot because they belong to the same family and can suffer from the same diseases.

3. *The pea/bean plot* Maincrop peas and beans take up a lot of space. On the other hand they produce prolifically and people, as a result, often grow many more of them than they need. So I have also allocated a large area (two full rows) to marrows, cucumber, sweet corn, etc., but if you want to grow more peas and beans (for example, French *petit pois*, which take up a lot of space and are not very prolific) there is no reason why the marrows should not be grown in one of the other plots. Or you might decide that hardy peas are a bit of a waste of time and effort – in which case you could sow spinach and seakale beet the previous year, following early potatoes. They would then go to seed in April or May and be lifted to make way for more beans or peas.

4. *The roots and onion plot* Leeks will overwinter and be harvested by June. Garlic will also be overwintered from November onwards. In milder areas most root crops can stay in the ground until they are required, and so long as they do not come to any harm this simplifies matters – unless you have ample vermin-proof storage space, or a large freezer. All root crops sprout into life the following spring, some of them producing useful green crops that can keep you supplied until summer crops begin to appear in late May or June, providing that they do not get in the way of your summer brassicas.

5. There are a number of 'fertile band' crops that do not fit into any of these groups and which can be grown anywhere, according to where you have space available, though, as I said above, it is better to grow them with the same group each year so that they share the benefits of the rotation. The most important are:

Celery and celeriac Celery needs an exceptionally rich soil to do well and (unless you are expert enough to grow your own plants from seed) it is as well to have a row trenched and prepared in readiness for the young plants when they make their brief appearance in the shops.

Spinach and seakale beet These are best grown as winter crops, occupying the ground from late summer until the following May.

Jerusalem artichokes These are usually grown in a permanent bed because (*a*) there is the temptation to adopt the myth that they will grow anywhere and, consequently, relegate them to some dismal outlying patch unfit for other crops, and (*b*) because of the insistent determination of every small piece of tuber to cling to life, making it quite difficult to eradicate them. This is a pity because artichokes do much better if they are planted with care in a well-

Figure 34: Planning your rotation using pieces of card (shaded green)

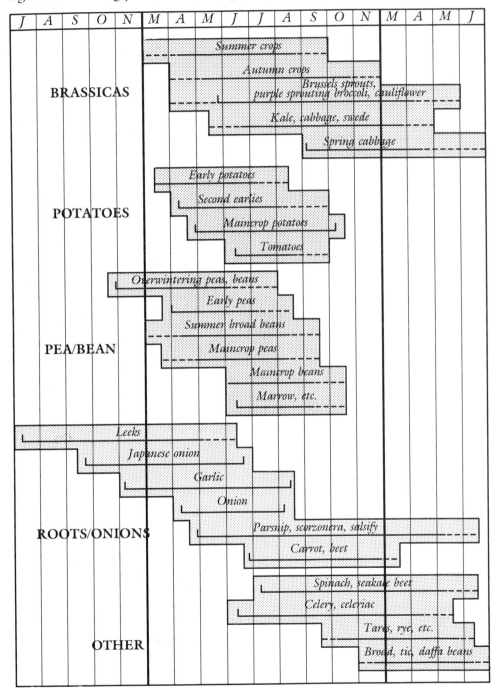

composted soil. Leaving them to fend for themselves in some desolate swampy spot accounts for some of the poor quality tubers produced, and the undeserved lack of popularity of this vegetable.

Marrow, courgette and cucumber These take up a lot of space and it is best to allocate two adjacent rows to them. The same applies to *sweet corn*, which is best grown in a box than in a row.

6. *Green manure crops* For most people the leguminous crops are the most worthwhile and they can make an important contribution to the fertility of the soil. Obviously if we are to preserve a strict rotation, leguminous green manure crops should coincide with the pea and bean year, that is with the overwintering broad beans and hardy peas. But here I would be inclined to agree with Allan Jackson (see page 98) and stretch a point: the legumes (peas and beans) are less susceptible than other crops in the rotation to soil-borne pests and diseases, so I feel that green manure crops (leguminous or otherwise) can either precede or follow (or both) the pea/bean year. Green manure crops can follow summer crops, some of them being sown as late as November. The benefit of green manure crops is greatly enhanced if they are left growing till May.

7. There is always the possibility that we shall have to trench one plot each year. Let us hope we do not have to, but we must not overlook the possibility.

This plan of mine, as you can see, is not a blueprint but merely an example which I have used to illustrate the way to go about planning a rotation to suit your own needs. If you have problems in deciding on the best order, it is worth making some diagrams of the four groups and of the green manure crop. It is quite a good idea to put the crops you propose to grow on a piece of card and cut them out as shown in Figure 34. You can then juggle these around to produce the best fit.

Throughout this chapter we will continue to use the order I proposed, that is brassicas, then potato and green manures, then pea/bean and green manures, then onion/roots, then brassicas. In the process of working it out you will gain familiarity and experience with the process of rotation so that you will be able to work out your own rotation with the crops you want to grow. However, no matter what order you choose, in a four-year rotation none of the four groups can be grown on more than a quarter of the available land, and this accounts for the limitations and inflexibility. It affects particularly the two groups that are most widely grown and which are also the most susceptible to disease – brassicas and potatoes. Very few people are likely to fill their allotments with onions or carrots, but there are quite a number who use them principally for growing their year's supply of potatoes, and very many of us who want to use more than a quarter of the area to grow brassicas. Sprouts, cauliflowers, sprouting broccoli, cabbages – these are the staple winter vegetables and they take up a lot of room. But in a four-year rotation you can only use a quarter of your land for potatoes and a quarter of it for brassicas. If you do not want to grow so many potatoes you will have a lot of empty space in your potato plot, but you must not fill it up with brassicas even though you may feel that the space given to them is too restricted. Nor should you fill the space with peas or beans or any of the onion crop – that is, you must not do so if you want to stick to a strict four-year rotation. However, there are two ways in which you can improve the situation: the first is obvious – you do all you can to make the plot's brassica year as productive as possible. Secondly, you reduce the number of permanent crops to a minimum. I think it is clear that the more crops you can bring into the rotation rather than remaining permanently on one site, the more space you have for your rotating crops. And in fact most 'permanent' crops benefit from being moved periodically; for example, it is wise to move your strawberry bed at least every three or four years, and the same applies to a number of crops that are frequently grown in the same bed year after year, such as Jerusalem artichokes (see pages 133–139 for more details).

As we plan our rotation we shall make use of a four-year diagram. Before we fill it in it is worth looking at the best type of diagram to use. Remember that we aim to do two things: the first is to plan in detail what crops we are going to grow this year and where we are going to grow them, according to the plan explained in the previous chapter (see below).

The second is to bear in mind that next year plot 1 will become the potato plot, in the following year the pea/bean plot, and so on. We do not need to plan the next four years in detail now, but we do need to make sure that what we want to grow this year will fit into an overall plan for all the plots over the four-year rotation. For example, say that in one half-row of plot 2 we decide to grow a row of late sprouts. In Figure 35, the late sprouts are planted in late June and lifted in April the following year. Suppose we then follow this next year (the potato year) with maincrop pota-

toes, lifted in September/October. Bearing in mind that the year following (the third year) is the pea/bean year, we could follow the maincrop potatoes with hardy peas sown in November and lifted the following June. This could be followed by spinach beet to stand the winter and go to seed the following May. This is the roots/onion year so the spinach beet could be followed by winter beetroot sown in June and lifted for storage during the winter leaving the plot ready for brassicas again in year 5.

If you want to change the crops you grow, when you plant and harvest them has got to fit in with the timing of the crops that you will grow in that plot the following year. If they do not, then you must alter the crops for the following years. If at a later date you decide that you do not really think it is worth while growing hardy peas, then either you must follow maincrop potatoes in year 2 with some other pea/bean crop that will be out of the ground by July in year 3 (such as broad beans), or by winter vegetables (such as over-wintering lettuce, which can be planted out at this time in a mild autumn or if you have some protection), or you could plant green manures. If, however, you wanted to leave it empty so that you could sow another half-row of maincrop peas next year, then you would have to find somewhere else for your spinach beet in year 3 because that would clash with your pea crop.

As you plan your crops for each plot you should keep a record by entering this on your diagram. You can, of course, have a separate diagram for each plot, but it is easier to combine these on one diagram for the whole area; the

	Plot 1	Plot 2	Plot 3	Plot 4
Year 1	A Brassicas	B Potatoes	C Peas/beans	D Roots/onions

Figure 35: One half of Plot 2 over the four year-rotation

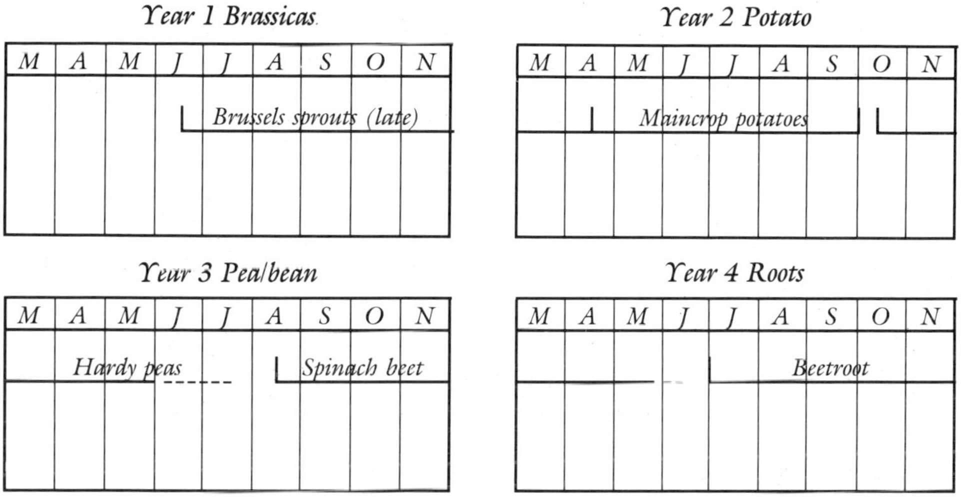

Year 1 Brassicas

M	A	M	J	J	A	S	O	N
				Brussels sprouts (late)				

Year 2 Potato

M	A	M	J	J	A	S	O	N
				Maincrop potatoes				

Year 3 Pea/bean

M	A	M	J	J	A	S	O	N
	Hardy peas				Spinach beet			

Year 4 Roots

M	A	M	J	J	A	S	O	N
					Beetroot			

only disadvantage is that this requires a rather large piece of paper. If you can get hold of some computer-print-out paper, this is ideal. Draw vertical lines down the page to give you the nine columns for the nine growing months of the year (March, April, May, June, July, August, September, October, November, abbreviated to MAMJ-JASON) four times to cover the four years. In the left margin, write each row, leaving space in between that you can use to record the intercropping rows. If you are going to divide each row into two halves (15 feet (4.6m) each for a normal allotment) you start with one half of each row (1a, 2a, 3a, etc.) and put the other half (1b, 2b, etc.) below it, as in Figure 36. It is worthwhile taking several photocopies of this blank diagram to save you having to draw it up again in the future. Each adjacent plot follows on across the paper. The whole four-year diagram is used for the completed rotation shown in Figure 37.

I hope it is clear after our discussion of diagrams previously that this diagram can either represent the four adjacent plots (brassicas, potatoes, peas/beans, roots/onions) for one year, or the history of one plot's rotation over the four years, and that, in constructing it, one has to bear in mind both of these factors.

We are now able to consider the choice of crops we are going to grow in our first year. Initially we will concentrate on the main crops that will, with a few exceptions, be grown in the fertile bands. We can no longer accept any old list – for example, the choices we made in Chapter 9, where nearly half the plot was planted with brassicas of one sort or another, because we are constrained by the need to fit each group into a quarter of the garden or allotment.

Plot 1: brassicas
Here is a provisional list of brassica crops – provisional because we may find we have to modify it later to fit everything in:

- 2 rows early sprouts
- 1½ rows late sprouts
- 2 rows cauliflower (5–7 plants each of three different varieties that crop at different times)

Figure 36: Diagram for one plot in a four-year rotation

	BRASSICA PLOT/YEAR									POTATO PLOT/YEAR . .			
	M	*A*	*M*	*J*	*J*	*A*	*S*	*O*	*N*	*M*	*A*	*M*	*J* . . . .
1a													
2a													
3a													
4a													
5a													
6a													
1b													
2b													
3b													
4b													
5b													
6b													

Note: If you blank out 'Brassica plot/year' and 'Potato plot/year' and photocopy this page four times, you can join the four copies together horizontally to make a blank diagram which you can use to plan the whole of your rotation

2 rows purple sprouting broccoli (one early, one late)

½ row kale

⅔ row swede ⎫
⅔ double row turnips ⎬ these three crops share
⅔ row Chinese cabbage ⎭ two rows

2 rows various cabbages and Savoy cabbage

2 rows spring cabbage

Note that from now on one row means one 15 foot (4.6m) row, which is half a full row across your garden or allotment. You will notice that we have fourteen rows of crops and only twelve rows to fit them into. We are able to do this because cabbages do not really need a whole 31 inch (80 cm) width to grow in, so we can grow spring cabbages here as an intermediate crop which fits quite well as spring cabbage does not need to be planted in very fertile ground – what it does need is an input of nitrogen in the spring to hasten it into growth. Also, through the winter it will remain quite a small plant and therefore will not interfere with the crops growing in the main rows on either side of it.

Exactly which crop you grow in which row will depend a bit on how well kept your garden or allotment is when you start; but I am going to assume that you are starting from scratch. I have put the turnips and cabbages in the outer rows because if you put them between the large brassicas they are liable to get overshadowed. When we come to fit in our summer brassicas we will find that the space between the rows of turnips and swede, and also between the swedes and the edge of the plot will be useful for late summer/autumn crops, though this depends upon the crops you are growing in adjacent plots.

There are no special points to remember for the other brassicas except when you come to transplanting them – for these, see page 66. On the diagrams I have marked brassicas for planting out at the beginning of July so as to leave room for early summer crops, but, if the rows are vacant, the earlier planting out can be done the better, so long as the transplants are ready to be moved.

This is especially important in the case of winter cauliflowers which, if they are planted out late in a very dry summer, may be in danger of forming tiny, immature heads in August (known as 'buttoning'). Once winter brassicas are planted out you can leave them to take care of themselves, except of course that plants are never free from the danger of diseases or disaster, so keep an eye open for slugs, caterpillars, aphids and pigeons, and watch out (especially after high winds) that they are not showing signs of keeling over. If they are, support them by earthing them up or staking them, or better still stake them before they actually keel over. These crops have been marked in on the first year of Figure 37.

Plot 2: potato and tomato

It is important not to forget that, although we are planning this year's potato plot, our plan must also be applicable to next year when the potatoes will be grown in plot 1, following the brassicas. Obviously some of the overwintering brassicas just marked in on the plan will still be *in situ* through the spring, and this must be taken into account when planning your potato-year crops. These are the crops I suggest we grow:

2 rows early potatoes

2 rows second earlies

4 – 6 rows maincrop potatoes

1 or 2 rows outdoor tomatoes

1 or 2 rows celery and/or celeriac

4 rows autumn-sown broad beans

1 or 2 rows early hardy peas

Figure 37: Diagram of main crops in a four-year rotation

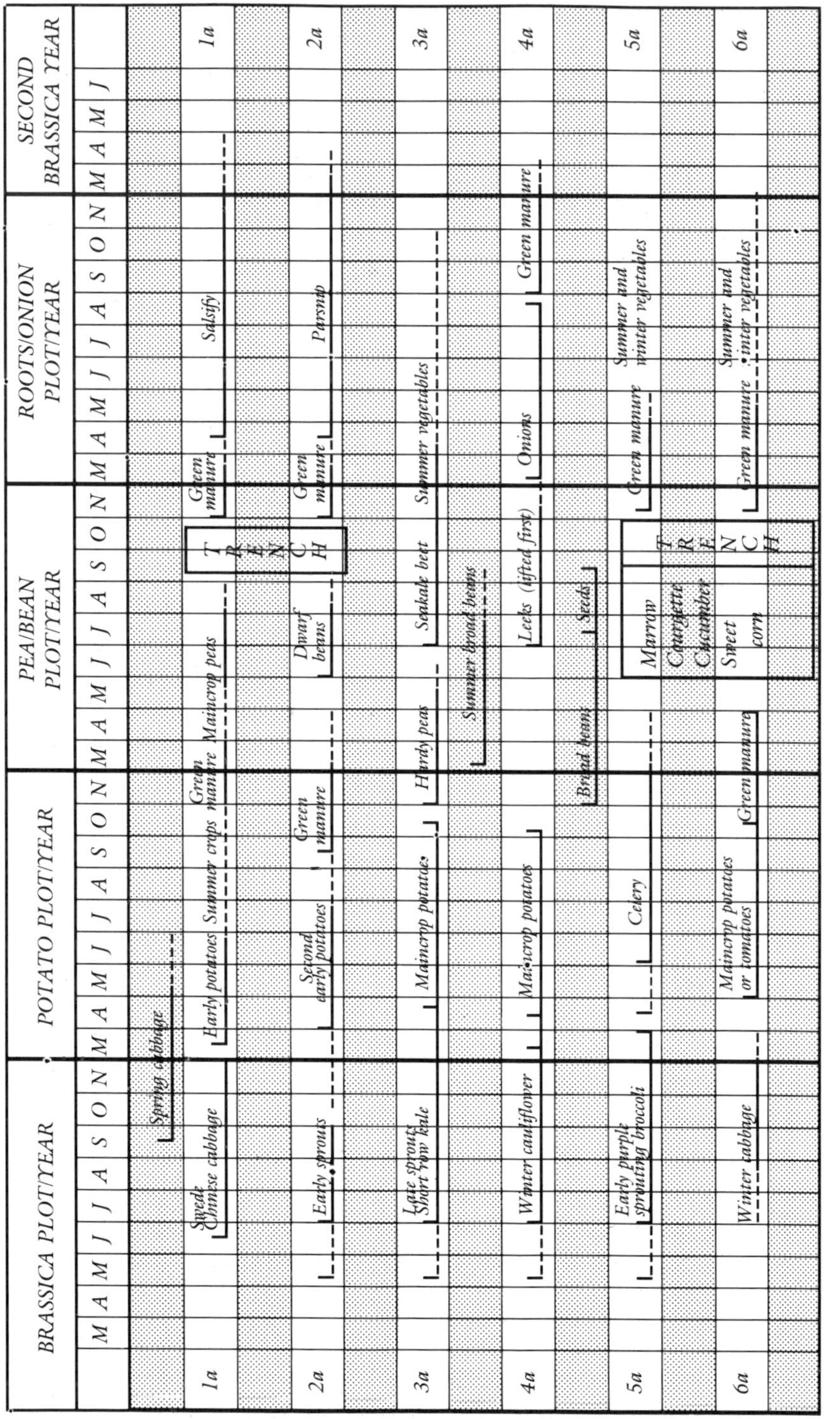

Column headings (left to right): BRASSICA PLOT/YEAR | POTATO PLOT/YEAR | PEA/BEAN PLOT/YEAR | ROOTS/ONION PLOT/YEAR | SECOND BRASSICA YEAR

Row labels: 1a, 2a, 3a, 4a, 5a, 6a

BRASSICA PLOT/YEAR:
- Spring cabbage
- Sweet Chinese cabbage
- Early sprouts
- Late sprouts / Short raw kale
- Winter cauliflower
- Early purple sprouting broccoli
- Winter cabbage

POTATO PLOT/YEAR:
- Early potatoes — Summer crops — Green manure
- Second early potatoes — Green manure
- Maincrop potatoes
- Maincrop potatoes
- Celery
- Maincrop potatoes or tomatoes — Green manure

PEA/BEAN PLOT/YEAR:
- Maincrop peas — Green manure — TRENCH
- Dwarf beans — Green manure
- Seakale beet
- Summer broad beans — Hardy peas
- Leeks (lifted first)
- Broad beans — Seeds
- Marrow / Courgette / Cucumber — TRENCH
- Sweet corn

ROOTS/ONION PLOT/YEAR:
- Salsify
- Parsnip
- Summer vegetables
- Onions — Green manure
- Green manure — Summer and winter vegetables
- Green manure — Summer and winter vegetables

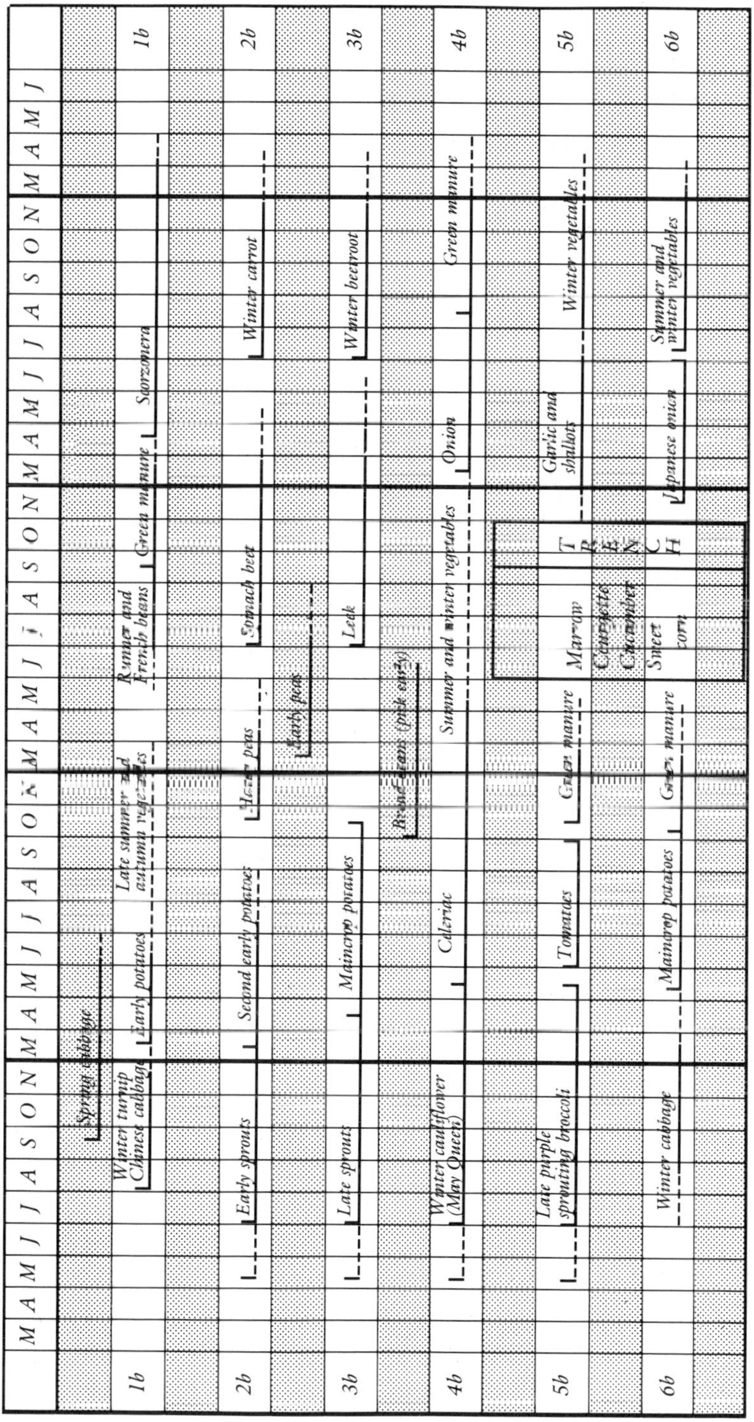

Top row labels: 1b, 2b, 3b, 4b, 5b, 6b

Month columns: M A M J J A S O N M A M J J A S O N M A M J J A S O N M A M J J

Crops by strip:

1b — Spring cabbage · Winter turnip, Chinese cabbage · Early potatoes · Late summer and autumn vegetables · Runner and French beans · Green manure · Scorzonera

2b — Early sprouts · Second early potatoes · Maize peas · Early peas · Spinach beet · Winter carrot

3b — Late sprouts · Maincrop potatoes · Broad beans (pick early) · Leek · Winter beetroot

4b — Winter cauliflower (May Queen) · Celeriac · Summer and winter vegetables · Onion · Green manure

5b — Late purple sprouting broccoli · Tomatoes · Green manure · Marrow · Courgette · Cucumber · Garlic and shallot · Winter vegetables

6b — Winter cabbage · Maincrop potatoes · Green manure · Japanese onion · Summer and winter vegetables

T R E N C H · Sweet corn

Bottom row labels: 1b, 2b, 3b, 4b, 5b, 6b

You may not wish to grow all these crops of potatoes, though the flavour of organically grown ones is so much superior to that of most shop-bought ones that it is worth it if you have the space, and for the same reason it is worth feeding the potato rows with as much compost as you can spare.

The best way to grow potatoes is to use small tubers that have been sprouted for at least a month. Limit them to two sprouts per tuber (pinching out others that grow) and plant them about 4 inches (10cm) deep in double rows 7 inches (18cm) apart in the fertile band, 8–12 inches (20–30cm) apart in the rows. Each tuber will produce a smaller crop than the normal, large, widely-spaced tubers, but the total crop will be about the same. The advantage of this method is that the earthing up required is minimal, so the space between the fertile bands need not be disturbed and can be used for intercropping.

The problem is getting hold of suitable seed potatoes. It is easy if you are using your own saved seed, but for bought seed you usually do not get much choice; you have to take what is available. You can cut larger tubers down to size, but this does not give such a good crop. Perhaps it is worth doing this initially to try the method out and then making a big effort to find a suitable source of smaller tubers if you decide to continue with it.

I think it is worth taking a risk and planting at least half a row of earlies at the beginning of March and, if you have no cloches, protecting them with straw. These tubers should be medium to small in size with no more than three shoots per potato; if they are too small they will not have enough plant food to enable them to recover if they are hit by frost. If you are lucky with the weather you will get a small crop, but one worth harvesting, by mid- or even early-May.

We will now go through the rows one by one to check the position next year when the potatoes follow the brassicas in plot 1:

Rows 1a, 2a, 1b and 2b The ground should have been cleared of the previous brassica crop though there may be a few swedes left. These should be lifted and stored.

Rows 3a, 4a, 3b Late sprouts will be lifted in April, ready for maincrop potatoes. Kale can also be lifted then, but if you want to keep it in for the lean months ahead, until it goes to seed, it can be followed by other crops, for example tomatoes in June.

Row 4a Cauliflowers will be cleared by early April (later ones are in row 4b).

Row 4b Cauliflower May Queen will be lifted by the beginning of June, to be followed by celeriac.

Row 5a Early purple sprouting broccoli will have been lifted by April, giving you plenty of time to prepare the ground for planting out celery in June.

Row 5b Late purple sprouting broccoli will be cleared in May, to make way for tomatoes in June.

Rows 6a, 6b These will be cleared by mid April though there may be the odd winter cabbage. There will also be intercropping spring cabbages, but these will not get in the way of planting potatoes in the main rows. They will be over by the time the potatoes begin to show growth above the ground. Or you may prefer to use these rows for tomatoes or other crops.

The following year will be your pea and bean year, so in the autumn you must sow your overwintering peas and beans. These can follow either your maincrop or your early potatoes; if they follow the earlies it should allow you time to fit in a quick-growing summer crop after you have lifted the earlies.

Broad beans are usually grown in double rows to simplify staking. As overwintered beans do not need too rich a soil (or they make too much growth, which will suffer in winter frosts) they can be sown in double rows 8 inches (20cm) apart between your fertile bands. This will leave 24 inches (61cm) between the rows. If the beans are carefully supported by stakes and trained, holding the stems in place with string, this will leave you room to plant or sow your fertile band next year while the bean crop is still in the ground. You will of course have to be careful where you tread when you are picking them. It is worth having two double rows, partly because there is no other crop that can follow maincrop potatoes and partly because, although it is not quite the tastiest of vegetables (summer broad beans are a different matter), it is a very welcome herald of spring in late May. I say late May because if you have two double rows you can afford to pinch out one of them after two or three flower-trusses to get very early crops. You can also pick the whole pods during May when they are no more than 2–3 inches (5–7cm) long for cooking and eating whole, and they are quite good raw in a crunchy salad.

Autumn-sown broad beans can also be valuable for green manure, in which case they should be sown 4–6 inches (10–15cm) apart each way within and between the fertile rows. But when you see the beans flowering in March or April you will be sorely tempted to let them all grow on to produce a crop and this must be resisted or you will not have enough space for next year's crops. Cut the green manure for compost as you need the ground, and only leave the rows that are planned to produce a crop. Naturally, if you are following a strict four-year rotation this is the autumn when you should be sowing leguminous green manure crops of all kinds, so that no part of the plot should be without some leguminous crop throughout the winter (except the celery and celeriac rows). Other beans such as tic or daffa or field beans are equally good for this. As a general rule, if your ground is free by September, sow winter tares, or a mixture of winter tares and winter rye-grass; and if it is not free until after that, sow beans of one sort or another. In all cases it is an advantage to pre-germinate the seeds to ensure germination if the weather turns wet and cold, and to minimize the time the seed lies at the mercy of mice and birds.

Autumn-sown peas are not heavy croppers so it is worth planting two rows. This will take a lot of seed for a small crop so it is worth saving seed from previous crops. As it flowers earlier than any other pea crop there is no danger of cross-pollination.

Plot 3: pea and bean
At its start you will have in the ground possibly some late celery or celeriac, and your rows of autumn-sown broad beans and peas. You will also have green manure that will have grown substantially – that is to say they will become huge during April and May if they remain in the ground that long. You will probably go on picking at least one of the double bean rows until July, and you may also leave some of the row in until August for seed. For a 30 foot (9m) row you will need at least a pint (0.5l) of seed, so it is well worth saving, especially if you also use broad beans as a green manure crop. Save seed every year as broad bean seed does not keep very well for longer periods of time. Be careful not to keep any seed that looks

the least bit diseased (for instance with small black marks or holes) as the seeds can transmit disease to next year's crop. Do not forget that bean plants cross-pollinate, so if you want a pure strain you must not sow more than one of the varieties that will flower simultaneously.

The crops we will be growing in the fertile band this year are as follows:

1 – 2 rows early peas
2 – 3 rows maincrop peas and beans of various sorts
1 row summer broad beans
1 or 2 rows summer veg (possibly)
2 rows seakale and spinach beet
2 double rows leeks
4 rows marrow/courgette/cucumber/ sweet corn
1 row garlic and/or ⎫
1 row shallots ⎬ in the autumn
1 row Japanese onion ⎭

Do not sow all the peas and beans at once in the spring; sow them in two or even three batches. If you save seed and therefore have plenty, take a risk. For example, start your runner bean plants off indoors and plant them out in early or mid May (depending on where you live). If they survive late frosts, pinch them out when they are about 4 feet (120cm) tall, and you will astonish your friends (and yourself) by getting very early crops. Have another lot coming along to replace them with if they are decimated by late frost.

With regard to the other main summer crops, these are spread over four rows, because marrows and so on will take up a lot of room, and sweetcorn are better planted in a block over two rows (including between the rows). They will not be planted out until early June so they can follow overwintered peas or celery or celeriac.

The following year an area will be planted with onions so you need to take account of this when deciding on the crops you sow this year for overwintering. Principally these will be leeks, which should, if possible, be planted out in late June or July. Depending on whether you like lots of small leeks or fewer big ones, you may plant them in a double row 7 inches (8cm) apart with 9 inches (23cm) between the plants, staggering them, or a double row with as little as 4 inches (10cm) between the plants or a triple row, 4 inches (10cm) between the rows and 6 inches (15cm) between the plants. Leeks are a very tough and trouble-free crop, and therefore people tend to treat them with scant care, but it is worth taking a little trouble to get the best crop from this excellent vegetable and for this you should follow the general directions given for transplanting on page 67.

Leeks grow best in a well-composted soil. As they are usually planted out by dibbing holes 4–6 inches (10–15cm) deep it is a good idea to loosen the soil to this depth, adding and mixing in some compost towards the bottom. It is also worth watering the surface of the ground before making the holes: this helps to prevent soil running back into the holes as you make them.

Good onions to grow the following year are the Japanese onions because they will mature in early July just when onions are expensive in the shops, and they are out of the ground early enough to enable you to follow with the summer crops next year. They are far easier to grow from sets than from seed and the sets may be planted up to early October, so they can follow the last of the summer vegetables.

Plant them in a double row 3 inches (7cm) apart in the row, unless you prefer large onions in which case plant them 4 or 5 inches (10 or 13cm) apart, though the closer planting will probably give you a more prolific crop.

Japanese onions do not keep well, so you should only plant sufficient to see you through the last two months of the summer before your main onion crop is ready.

You will notice that maincrop peas in row 1a overlap green manure crops. This means that where you want to plant the maincrop early (for example, half or a third of a row of peas sown in March, perhaps another third in April, and so on) you must be quite ruthless in removing the green manure crops. They are there to fill up space profitably rather than leave it empty, they do not have any squatters' rights when an edible crop is needed.

You will also notice that I have marked in spaces where you may have time for trenching, if it is needed, but I have not managed to fit in all the rows, so, if you think the soil is in real need of it, you must make a note to fit it in the missing rows another time.

Plot 4: roots and onion
Now for our last plot – here are the crops:

1 double row Japanese onions, sown last autumn
1 row garlic, sown last autumn
1 row shallots, sown last autumn
2 rows leeks, sown last summer
2 double rows onions
1 double row parsnips
1 double row salsify
1 double row scorzonera
1 double row winter beetroot
1 double or triple row winter carrots

If you decide to grow Jerusalem artichokes in your rotation rather than in a permanent bed, which is what I recommend, they could follow the green manure in row 5a or 6a.

The overwintering crops that remain in the ground after March are salsify, scorzonera, parsnips and artichokes. Next year will be another brassica year

and if you want to use any of these rows for early summer brassicas you can do so by practising a little ingenuity. For example, you will probably have lifted at least half a row of each of these root crops by the middle of March. If you are planting out, say, early cauliflowers or cabbages you can plant them in these empty half rows at double the usual density and then move half of them again as the rest of the rows become free. This late transplanting will not harm the plants if the method described on page 65 is followed. Alternatively you can lift the root crops and store them, leaving the whole row free.

Salsify roots become inedible after the plant starts going to seed but you can leave salsify to grow on until the green leafy tops appear, as the tops can be eaten either green or blanched. Although good, I cannot honestly claim, as some people do, that it is a succulent substitute for asparagus. Scorzonera roots, however, remain edible for the whole year. You will need to support the flower heads if you want to collect the seed though, as the stems are not very firmly rooted and have a tendency to keel over. It is a perennial and its roots will continue to grow so it is well worth letting a few do so for the lean months of May and June when root vegetables are at a premium.

Salsify and scorzonera germinate quite quickly but randomly, especially if the seed is over one year old, so it is worth pre-germinating them and only sowing those seeds that show definite signs of life. They can be sown 6 inches (15cm) apart in 7 inch (18cm) rows – though if you intend to grow scorzonera on to get bigger roots you can grow them farther apart still. Do not forget that both these roots, especially scorzonera, plunge down a long way into the earth so, if you do not want to waste half the crop by breaking the roots when you are trying to dig them up, you should ensure that the soil is fairly loose: it is worth loosening it to at least a spade's depth (though the roots grow much deeper than that) and mixing in some fine compost. Alternatively, if you have an intractable soil you should use the crow-bar method, which, I have found, is the best way to prepare the ground for any of the root crops, even carrots: you make a conical hole with a crow-bar, or for smaller crops, like carrots or small parsnips, a v-shaped slit along the whole row and fill it with finely sieved compost. Do this a month before sowing if you can so that the compost will settle, and mark each hole with a stick. Top it up after a fortnight. When you come to sow, sow two pre-germinated seeds on the surface (that will have sunk once again) and cover it with fine, damp soil. Of course this method is slightly contrary to the idea of smaller individual crops, for making and filling ninety holes in hard, clayey ground is a daunting prospect, but it is a way to get very good, clean crops.

In the old days we sowed parsnips in February about 18 inches (46cm) apart, aiming to produce huge roots but these were usually sorely afflicted with canker so that half of them had to be cut away. Now the trend is for later sowing, closer planting and much smaller, cleaner crops.

Parsnips take a long time to germinate and often get lost in and smothered by the weeds that grow fast and vigorously in the spring sunshine. It is, therefore, worthwhile (and very easy) to pre-germinate parsnip seeds. Sow them in a double row 7 inches (18cm) apart and thin to 4 inches (10cm) apart – staggering them in the rows – and you will get 90 parsnips per row to last you from November to March – enough to make anyone long for the summer!

There is a lot to be said for sowing maincrop carrots in late June or July so as to avoid the worst carrot-fly invasion in June/July, though they will not miss the ravages of the September visitation.

Now, our diagram for the whole plot is complete and can be used without alteration for each subsequent year of the rotation – indeed, for the indefinite future. Most people will want to change and experiment, growing a variety of different crops over the years. This is not a problem as the diagram can be used as a basic foundation, always remembering that any change in one year will need to be followed through for subsequent years.

If you compare this diagram with the one we produced in Chapter 4 (page 52, Figure 14), you will see the sort of restrictions the four-year rotation enforces on what we can grow. In our half-allotment in Chapter 4 we grew twelve winter brassica crops, and nine other winter crops, making a total of twenty-one rows out of twenty-four producing edible crops through the winter (nearly 90 per cent productivity). With the four-year rotation plan we are producing twelve winter brassica crops and fourteen others, a total of twenty-six rows out of a total of forty-eight, only just over fifty per cent productivity. Of course this is not a fair comparison because in this rotation we have included nine rows of potatoes, a summer only crop, that we did not grow at all in our earlier plan, and we have grown quite a few green manure crops, which we also had hardly any room for previously. It is, however, too soon to carry out such a final assessment as we still have a lot of crops to fit in, mainly summer crops but also including a number of smaller winter crops that did not belong to any of the rotation groups.

CHAPTER 12
FOUR-YEAR ROTATION – THE OTHER CROPS

The summer crops are not difficult to explain now because many of the problems and possibilities have been looked at in previous Chapters. An important point to remember when planning crops in advance is that each year plots 1 and 4 will be on the outer edges of your growing area. Assuming that you have left a reasonable amount of space beyond the outermost fertile rows, there will be room for intercropping rows at each end. For this reason I have shown space on Figure 37 above row 1 and also below row 6. Where two plots adjoin each other though, they share this space, so it is important to take care not to double-book it. For example in the diagram, in year 1 the brassica plot will be at one end of the garden and row 1 will be on the outside, whereas the following year the brassica plot will rotate to the other end and then row 6 will be the outside row. This also means that in year 1, row 6 of the brassica year will adjoin row 1 of the potato plot and so the intercropping row below row 6 of the brassicas and the intercropping row above row 1 of the potatoes is the same row. You can use this for one or the other plot but you cannot use it for both. There is another point, and that is that the potato plot this year was growing brassicas last year, and if last year you used the intercropping row above row 1 to grow an overwintering crop (for example, spring cabbage, as shown in

the diagram) then this crop will still be there at the beginning of this year. In the case of spring cabbage, it will remain there until June or July – so whatever crop you decide to put in that space will have to follow the cabbages, as they are lifted.

We will now take each plot in turn, referring to Figure 38. The crops we have already decided on for the main rows, as shown in Figure 37, are repeated here in black. The intercropping rows we are now considering are shown in green.

Plot 1: brassicas
I have marked the main crops to be planted out at the end of June, but it is quite satisfactory to delay this until at least mid July if you use the methods described on pages 65 – 66. This will enable you to grow summer brassicas in these rows, lifting first the ones that occupy the rows for the main crop, as shown in Figure 38. Summer crops can also be grown between the rows until early August. This does not contradict our decision that these rows should be left undisturbed for several weeks before planting out the winter crops in order to allow the soil to consolidate because the presence of a summer crop with the plants spaced 31 inches (80cm) apart will not prevent this consolidation – in fact it will help to ensure that the soil is not disturbed. When you come to lift the summer crop it is better to cut

Figure 38: Diagram of main and summer crops (summer crops in green) in a four-year rotation

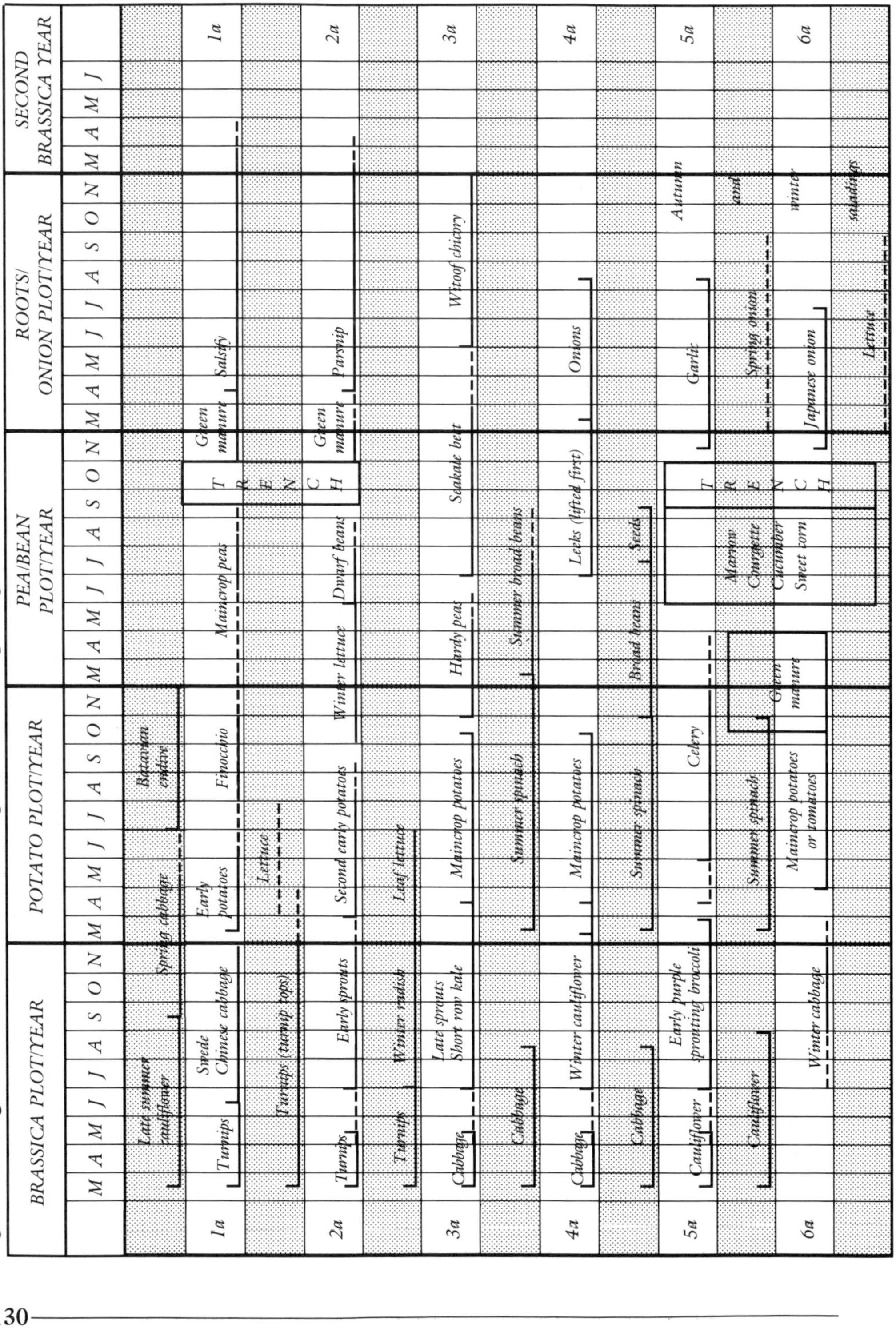

BRASSICA PLOT/YEAR	POTATO PLOT/YEAR	PEA/BEAN PLOT/YEAR	ROOTS/ONION PLOT/YEAR	SECOND BRASSICA YEAR
M A M J J A S O N	M A M J J A S O N	M A M J J A S O N	M A M J J A S O N M A M J	M A M J
Late summer cauliflower / Spring cabbage / Swede / Chinese cabbage	Batavian endive / Early potatoes / Finocchio / Lettuce	Maincrop peas / T R E N C H / Green manure / Salsify		1a
Turnips / Turnips (turnip tops)	Second early potatoes	Winter lettuce / Dwarf beans / Green manure / Parsnip		2a
Turnips / Early sprouts / Winter radish	Leaf lettuce / Maincrop potatoes	Hardy peas / Seakale beet / Witloof chicory		3a
Turnip / Late sprouts / Short row kale	Summer spinach / Maincrop potatoes	Summer broad beans / Leeks (lifted first) / Onions		4a
Cabbage / Winter cauliflower	Summer spinach / Celery	Broad beans / Seeds / Garlic / Spring onion / Autumn and winter		5a
Cabbage / Early purple sprouting broccoli	Green manure / Maincrop potatoes or tomatoes	Marrow / Courgette / Cucumber / Sweet corn / T R E N C H / Japanese onion / Lettuce seedlings		6a
Cauliflower / Cauliflower / Winter cabbage				

Month columns (top and bottom): M A M J J A S O N M A M J J A S O N M A M J J A S O N M A M J J A S O N M A M J J A S O N M A M J

Row labels: 1b, 2b, 3b, 4b, 5b, 6b

1b
Late summer cabbage · Spring cabbage · Winter turnip · Chinese cabbage · Early potatoes · Endive · Chicory · Runner and French beans · Scorzonera
Kohlrabi

2b
Kohlrabi · Early sprouts · Lettuce · Second early potatoes · Hardy peas · Summer carrot · Winter carrot
Kohlrabi

3b
Kohlrabi · Late sprouts · Leaf lettuce · Maincrop potatoes · Early peas · Spinach beet · Summer beetroot · Winter beetroot

4b
Winter cauliflower (May Queen) · Summer saladings · Celeriac · Broad beans (pick early) · Leeks · Winter beetroot

5b
Calabrese · Late purple sprouting broccoli · Summer saladings · Tomatoes · Broad beans · Marrow · Courgette, Cucumber, Sweetcorn · Onions · Garlic and shallots · Winter vegetables
Calabrese

6b
Calabrese · Winter cabbage · Maincrop potatoes · Green manure · Green manure · Japanese onion · Lettuce · and saladings

(Large boxed letters spanning rows 4b–5b: T R E N C H)

the stems below ground level (I use a sharp, saw-toothed knife for this) rather than pull or dig them up.

You may think that I have allocated rather too many rows for summer brassicas, but do not forget that, in practice, there will be several overwintered crops occupying many of these rows until March or April, which will limit the actual space available – see the right-hand end of Figure 38 under the heading 'Second brassica year': salsify, parsnip, scorzonera and possibly also artichoke will all still be occupying space, and so may several of the winter saladings. If you do not wish to grow summer cabbages, cauliflowers, etc., there is, of course, no reason why you should not use the space for other summer crops.

I have not marked in summer radish. It takes up so little space for such a short time that I do not think it is an important consideration. Winter radish (Black Spanish, China Rose, etc.) is another matter. They grow as large as turnips, or larger, and need the same spacing. A short row can intercrop between the kale and early sprouts (rows 2a/3a).

Autumn brassicas can only be grown at the expense of some of the winter crops. They are alternatives, and you have to choose between them.

A crop seldom grown nowadays but well worth growing is turnip tops (row 1a/2a). You sow turnips in September, thin them to 1–2 inches (2–5cm) apart and harvest them when they sprout in March to May. If you like strong-flavoured greens, you will like these and I am sure they are very nutritious.

Plot 2: potato

As I have said there will be quite a lot of uncertainty here, depending upon whether you wish to grow all or most of your own potatoes. In Figure 38 I have assumed that we do wish to grow a good proportion of them – that is, 2 rows of earlies, 2 of second earlies, and 4 or 5 maincrop. As you will remember from the previous Chapter, if you use small potatoes for seed, planted close together, the productivity will be about the same as is usual for the crop, but you will minimize the need for earthing up. This will allow you to grow crops between your rows of earlies and second earlies and, as you will see, I have planned to use this space for leaf lettuce and hearting lettuce. I suggest you choose small lettuces, like Little Gem or Lobjots, as larger lettuces can be grown in plot 4. I have not planned to intercrop our maincrop potatoes. Although it is perfectly feasible, it may be safer not to do so in the first year of the rotation, until you have had some experience of growing them this way and can feel confident enough to judge the matter for yourselves.

As I did not use the interspace below row 6 of the brassica plot it is available for cropping in the potato plot. I have used it for late summer and autumn endives, to follow the spring cabbages as they are lifted, though it could be used for any crop that is planted in June or later.

I have used the potato plot mainly for summer saladings. As finocchio is such a good vegetable, which needs to be sown through late June and July, and as it may be quite difficult to find space for it, I have decided to grow finocchio and other crops in rows 1a and 2a instead of green manures. I have retained the green manures in rows 5 and 6, but these may have to be sacrificed too if your cropping plan demands it. Obviously we must leave the intercrop row between row 6 of this plot and row 1 of the pea/bean plot empty because of the space needed for maincrop peas and beans in row 1 of the pea/bean plot.

Plot 3: pea/bean

The pea/bean plot is crowded: there is almost no room for intercropping and therefore little scope for experimenting with different varieties of peas and beans and even the maincrop peas and beans are short of space. If you feel you need more space I recommend that you move the seakale and spinach beet on to the roots/onion plot – remembering that they will overwinter until the following May, limiting the summer brassicas you will be able to grow there next year. Alternatively, they could be moved to the potato plot.

Plot 4: roots/onion

Root crops do not take up so much space, and this leaves plenty of room for intercropping. It is here many of the summer vegetables (apart from the brassicas of course) will be grown, followed by winter saladings, many of which are quite hardy. People often think that salad crops will not survive frosts and so they do not grow them in the winter, but both land cress and chicory rosso have survived very cold spells in my garden in the past, as did some French parsley. Although the French parsley remained leafless until March, the plants then sprouted up and went to seed – the curled parsley in contrast went on producing throughout the winter. Corn salad, witloof chicory and sorrel are also very hardy saladings.

I have not filled in the intercrops in rows 2a to 4a as there is such a wide choice here but I would probably use the space to grow several more rows of autumn and winter carrot and beetroot.

Summer green manure crops are quite difficult to plan and perhaps unnecessary because summer cropping is often decided on an *ad hoc* basis depending on how particular crops have done, the weather and other such unpredictable factors. Some guidelines though can be given, for example you can plant mustard in any interrows in the brassica year where you are not growing summer crops; fenugreek (which you can, in fact, harvest) alongside maincrop peas and beans, undersowing crops (growing with or after another crop) such as marrow and sweet corn.

There are several vegetables I have not mentioned so far: some of them (seakale, asparagus and Good King Henry) because they are perennials and will be catered for in the non-rotationary portion of your garden – but this will be discussed in the following pages.

When it comes to putting this plan into operation, you will be unlikely to want to grow all the crops shown and some may be better suited to your garden than others. Go through the list in Chapter 3, perhaps in conjunction with one or two seed catalogues, decide on your priorities, select crops bearing in mind your experience and abilities, and then perhaps add not more than three or four crops that you would like to try experimentally. Certainly for the first year or so I would omit the green manure, unless in your area it is virtually impossible to buy or find any organic manure. This is a very unlikely situation though – even in large cities horse manure is available, and often quantities of discarded vegetables from the street markets.

Obviously the more crops you manage to include in your rotation, the more room there will be for your crops – I am thinking especially of the overcrowded brassica year. For example, if we could incorporate four more full rows from our permanent bed we would have seven rows in each of our plots instead of six, and this would enable us, for example, to grow thirty or forty winter cauliflowers instead of fifteen or twenty. Fifteen cauliflowers throughout the season is not enough for the average family. In addition, if you feel rotation is a good idea, the more crops that benefit from it the better. However, be warned, an increased number of crops requires quite complicated planning and, unless you are fairly familiar with rotations and how to plan them, it might be quite confusing simply to read about it! I think it would be wise for beginners to stop here on the first reading and to proceed to the next few pages only when they are more practised at planning crop rotations.

Here are a few of the crops that might be brought into the rotation:

Asparagus Most people still grow this in the old-fashioned way in a permanent bed, and certainly in this book I have regarded it as a permanent crop. However, it is often now recommended that it be grown from seed in single rows and it is often grown commercially this way. This means that each year you sow one row (or rows) that remain asparagus row(s) for three or four years. In the fourth year the crop is harvested right through the season and lifted at the end of it. Meanwhile, further rows have been sown annually, so that each year a three- or four-year-old row comes to maturity, produces a crop, is harvested, is lifted and superceded by a new row. This means that three to four rows are devoted to asparagus, which is about the same space as a permanent asparagus bed will take up. That is a lot of room, but then you may feel that asparagus, 'the most delicious and esteemed of all vegetables' according to Vilmorin-Andrieux, the doyen of French gardening writers, is worth it. An added bonus is that it crops in May and June, just when nearly all other vegetables are unavailable.

Strawberries These are grown by most people in a semi-permanent bed that gradually becomes a matted tapestry of runners and weeds. It is better to plant new runners each year, leave them for two or possibly three years, and then grow replacement plants on a new site – and it is here that the discipline of a rotation does help you to keep up with these tasks, which are otherwise so easy to pass over, to overlook, or put off.

Rhubarb This is really only a marginal candidate for rotation as most people are of the opinion that it should remain in a permanent bed for several years, indeed for ever. However, it can be moved, and some people recommend it, and the move can be combined with detaching some crowns for forcing, but I doubt if there would be any benefit in moving it more often than every 5 or 6 years. Other crops that will continue to be productive over a period are: seakale, for five years (it is a brassica, though, and that might pose some problems); Good King Henry; sorrel, for five years or more; 'Nine-star Broccoli', a perennial that produces several heads (I am always a bit suspicious of these less straightforward varieties, but this one does produce exactly nine good heads, though they are small).

First of all we will look at how to incorporate strawberries into our rotation. I am going to assume that we grow a lot of strawberries and that, at present, our strawberry bed takes up four full rows. The first thing to do is to re-plan the plots so that the four strawberry rows are incorporated into them, giving you one extra row in each plot, that is seven rows in all. As in the previous chapter you can treat these as fourteen half-rows, but to keep the diagram down to a manageable size I am going to show them here as seven full rows. I am also going to assume that you are a keen consumer of potatoes and brassicas and that you aim to grow more of both these crops.

Your strawberries will always be planted in the year following brassicas (which, in our case, is the potato year), and will remain for three years and then be lifted after the crop has been harvested to clear the ground for seven rows of brassicas in the following year. Alternatively, they can be left in until the following year, cropped until mid July and then lifted to make way for the late-planted winter brassicas (cabbage, Chinese cabbage and turnip). The strawberry runners should be planted out by mid August and this means that they could follow a row of early potatoes. So our plot will provide the following:

In year 1: seven rows of potatoes, etc., then one row of strawberries planted in August after early potatoes.

In year 2: six rows of peas and beans, plus one row of strawberries, producing their first crop

In year 3: six rows of root crops, plus one row of strawberries producing their second year's crop (then, either lift the strawberries to make way for a late July sowing of winter roots (carrots or beetroot, for example) or retain them for another year)

In year 4: six rows of brassicas, plus one row of strawberries lifted in July and followed by July-planted brassicas, or, possibly lifted in August and followed by spring cabbage

This is shown in Figure 39.

You can see from this that in addition to a two- or three year crop of strawberries you are also gaining an extra row of both potatoes and winter brassicas.

Of course all this cannot be accomplished overnight. Unless you are going to forego strawberries for a year or so, there will have to be a transition period when you are gradually integrating your strawberries, row by row, into your rotation

Figure 39: Incorporating strawberries or asparagus into a four-year rotation

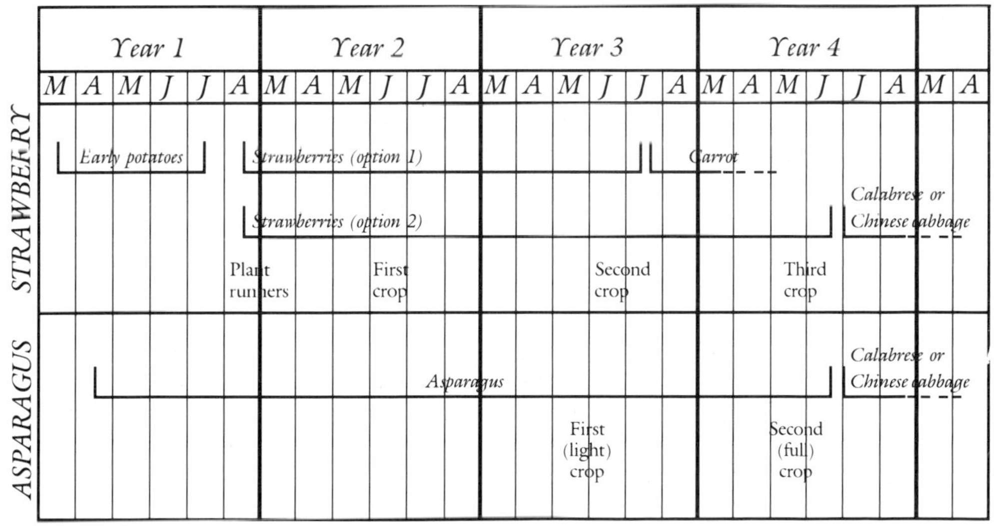

Figure 40: Four-year rotation for strawberries or asparagus worked out for sixteen years

Year	1	2	3	4	5	6	7	8	9	10	11	12	13	14	15	16
PLOT 1 Row 1		1	2	3	(4)					1	2	3	(4)			
Row 2	B				B				B				B			
Row 3	R				R				R				R			
Row 4	A				A				A				A			
Row 5	S				S	1	2	3	(4)S				S	1	2	3
Row 6	S				S				S				S			
Row 7																
PLOT 2 Row 1	1	2	3	(4)					1	2	3	(4)				
Row 2				B				B				B				B
Row 3				R				R				R				R
Row 4				A				A				A				A
Row 5				S	1	2	3	(4)S				S	1	2	3	S
Row 6				S				S				S				(4)S
Row 7																
PLOT 3 Row 1				1	2	3						1	2	3		
Row 2			B				(4)B				B				(4)B	
Row 3			R				R				R				R	
Row 4		2	3	(4)A			A				A				A	
Row 5			S				S	1	2	3	(4)S				S	1
Row 6			S				S				S				S	
Row 7																
PLOT 4 Row 1			1	2	3	(4)					1	2	3	(4)		
Row 2		B				B				B				B		
Row 3		R				R				R				R		
Row 4	3	(4)A				A				A				A		
Row 5		S				S	1	2	3	(4)S				S	1	2
Row 6		S				S				S				S		
Row 7																

Key:

Strawberries:

1 Plant runners in August, after early potatoes

2 First-year crop

3 Second-year crop, lifted and followed by August-sown root crop

(4) Strawberries may be left for a further year followed by a late-planted brassica crop

Asparagus:

Similar, but must be sown in spring of Year 1 and lifted in August of Year 4

Let us now see how this works out over the years. I am going to look at plot 2 of our rotation because it is the one in which potatoes are grown in year one, so it is here that we start with our first row of strawberries. Figure 40 is unlike our previous diagrams in which each unit across the top of the page represents one month of the growing season. Here we shall trace our rotation over several years so each unit represents one year. So we plant out our strawberries in year 1 and leave them *in situ* through years 2 and 3 and then lift them. (As explained above we can also leave them for a further season and lift them in year 4 if we wish, but in the figure I have shown the first option of lifting them in year 3.) Meanwhile in years 2, 3 and 4, our potato crop will be grown in plots 4, 3 and 1 so each year a new row of strawberries will be planted successively in those plots also. All this is shown in Figure 40. In year 5 our plot 2 will be growing potatoes again and we take care to grow earlies in row 5 and follow these once more with a new row of strawberries. From now on you will be planting a new row of strawberries every fourth year in each plot, and I suggest you adhere to the following order:

first year:	row 1
fifth year:	row 5
ninth year:	row 2
thirteenth year:	row 6
seventeenth year:	row 3
twenty-first year:	row 7
twenty-fifth year:	row 4
twenty-ninth year:	row 1 again, and so on.

As you can see from Figure 40, this order ensures that there is a six-year interval between lifting a crop and growing it again in an adjacent row. For example, the crop in row 1 is lifted in year 3 (or possibly year 4) and an adjacent crop in row 2 is not planted until year 9, five or six years later. Similarly a crop is not grown in the same row until twenty-six years after the previous crop is lifted (in row 1, the interval between year 3 and year 29).

Exactly the same procedure can be used for growing asparagus, with one exception. Asparagus is grown from seed sown in the spring so it cannot follow a row of early potatoes. Also, asparagus will not crop at all in its second year, and only sparsely in its third (though modern varieties are said to improve on older ones in this respect) so it is really essential to retain them for the fourth year before lifting them.

You can, of course, bring both asparagus and strawberries into your rotation and this will provide eight-row plots and give you an even longer interval between crops in the same row – thirty years to be exact – see Figure 41. Here I have placed the asparagus and strawberry rows side by side but this is not a necessity – the rows can be quite separate so long as they both follow the order given above: 1 – 5 – 2 – 6 – 3 – 7 – 4 – 8 – 1 – etc.

All this may seem rather complicated – is it worth it? For strawberries I would definitely say it is. It does help to keep them free from disease and it also saves you having a strawberry bed that soon becomes a tangled mess. The only disadvantage is that, with strawberry rows dotted here and there amongst your four plots, it may make netting a bit more difficult.

For asparagus, my answer is less definite. For me there has always been something almost mystical about the old-fashioned asparagus bed, rising up like a bronze-age barrow, and continuing to provide an asparagus crop for twenty years or so. The modern method may be, as it is claimed, more productive, but I cannot help feeling that it will

Figure 41: Four-year rotation for strawberres and asparagus together

	Year	1	2	3	4	5	6	7	8	9	10	11	12	13	14	15	16
	Row 1		1	2	3	4											
	2	B	1	2	3	B				B	1	2	3	4B			
PLOT 1	3	R				R				R	1	2	3	R			
	4	A				A				A				A			
	5	S				S	1	2	3	4S				S			
	6	S				S	1	2	3	S				S	1	2	3
	7														1	2	3
	8																
	1	1	2	3	4												
PLOT 2	2	1	2	3						1	2	3	4				
	3				B				B	1	2	3	B				B
	4				R				R				R				R
	5				A	1	2	3	4A				A				A
	6				S	1	2	3	S				S	1	2	3	4S
	7				S				S				S	1	2	3	S
	8																
	1				1	2	3	4									
	2			B	1	2	3	B				B	1	2	3	4B	
PLOT 3	3			R				R				R	1	2	3	R	
	4			A				A				A				A	
	5			S				S	1	2	3	4S				S	
	6			S				S	1	2	3	S				S	1
	7																1
	8																
	1			1	2	3	4										
	2		B	1	2	3	B				B	1	2	3	4B		
PLOT 4	3		R				R				R	1	2	3	R		
	4		A				A				A				A		
	5		S				S	1	2	3	4S				S		
	6		S				S	1	2	3	S				S	1	2
	7															1	2
	8																

Key:
1234 asparagus rotation
123   strawberry rotation

make redundant one of the main glories of the traditional garden.

I do not think it is worthwhile to attempt a similar system with rhubarb, which seems content to remain on the same site indefinitely. Moving it is quite an undertaking and, as most people do not wish to grow more than half a row altogether, it would be almost counter-productive to fit it into our rotation.

Seakale and nine-star broccoli, both productive for five years or so, present a problem because they are brassicas and thus would be liable to nullify the benefits of your rotation. If you are worried about club root they should perhaps be grown as far as possible from your vegetable garden, or at any rate from that part of it devoted to your rotation. Although nine-star broccoli might look a little out of place in the flower garden and perhaps be better hidden in some inconspicuous corner, seakale would look good there. It has attractive, crinkly, bluish-grey foliage and unusual white flowers (plants for cropping should not be allowed to flower but a few can be left to do so and to produce seed).

I think it is worth making a distinction between these two crops: nine-star broccoli is quite fun to grow but the crop it produces is not markedly different from or an improvement on other headed cauliflowers, except that the heads are smaller. Seakale, on the other hand, is a delicious and delicate vegetable and is unique in that it is indigenous to the British Isles. It is very difficult to find shops that sell it and so it will come very high on the lists of people who like to grow unusual, generally unavailable, expensive and epicurean vegetables.

CHAPTER 13
THREE-YEAR ROTATION

Having dealt with the planning of a four-year rotation in detail, the planning of a three-year one is practically self-evident. A three-year rotation involves having eight rows in each of three plots instead of the six rows in a four-year one. This gives us a lot more flexibility and make the exercise significantly easier. The main crops in a typical three-year rotation are shown in Figure 42. Note that all the onion crops (including leeks and garlic) are now on one side of the plot (that is, in the 'a' rows). So if we alternate the sides every three years by following the 'a' rows in the pea/bean year with the 'b' rows of the brassica year, and vice versa then, when the onions are next grown in this plot they too will all be in the 'b' rows. So, effectively, we have achieved a six-year rotation for onions. In theory you can achieve a six-year rotation in this way for any crop that does not occupy more than half the plot: what you do is to grow all the susceptible crops on one side of the plot in the first rotation, and ensure that they all switch to the other side for the second. In practice it is not always easy, but in Figure 43 I have shown a similar plan in which the potato crop has a six-year rotation. This could be very valuable if your potatoes are vulnerable to disease, but it is somewhat spoiled by the fact that tomatoes are grown on the other side of the plot, and thus either potatoes or tomatoes (both of which belong to

the solanaceae family and are therefore host to the same pests and diseases) will grow there every third year. There are two possible remedies for this. One is to reduce your potato rows or your tomato rows so that you only have eight rows of these two crops in all. The other possibility is to intercrop your tomatoes between the early or second-early potato rows. This is possible if you use small-seeded potatoes and in this way avoid having to earth up. But you will have to be very careful when you lift your potatoes not to disturb the young tomato plants between the potato rows.

You will find that with this selection of crops it is not possible for both the potatoes and the onions to rotate on a six-yearly basis in this way.

In the three-year rotation there is obviously not nearly so much pressure on the brassica year since eight rows give ample scope for a reasonable spread of crops. This makes it more practicable to precede your main brassica crops with green manure. Simply hoe the plants off at surface level when they show signs of going to seed. The green manure should have smothered any other weeds, so the ground should be suitable for planting without any further attention and, having been undisturbed since the autumn, it should be suitably firm for brassicas. But, as I have emphasized throughout the book, although I have marked in large areas of green manure, these will not normally

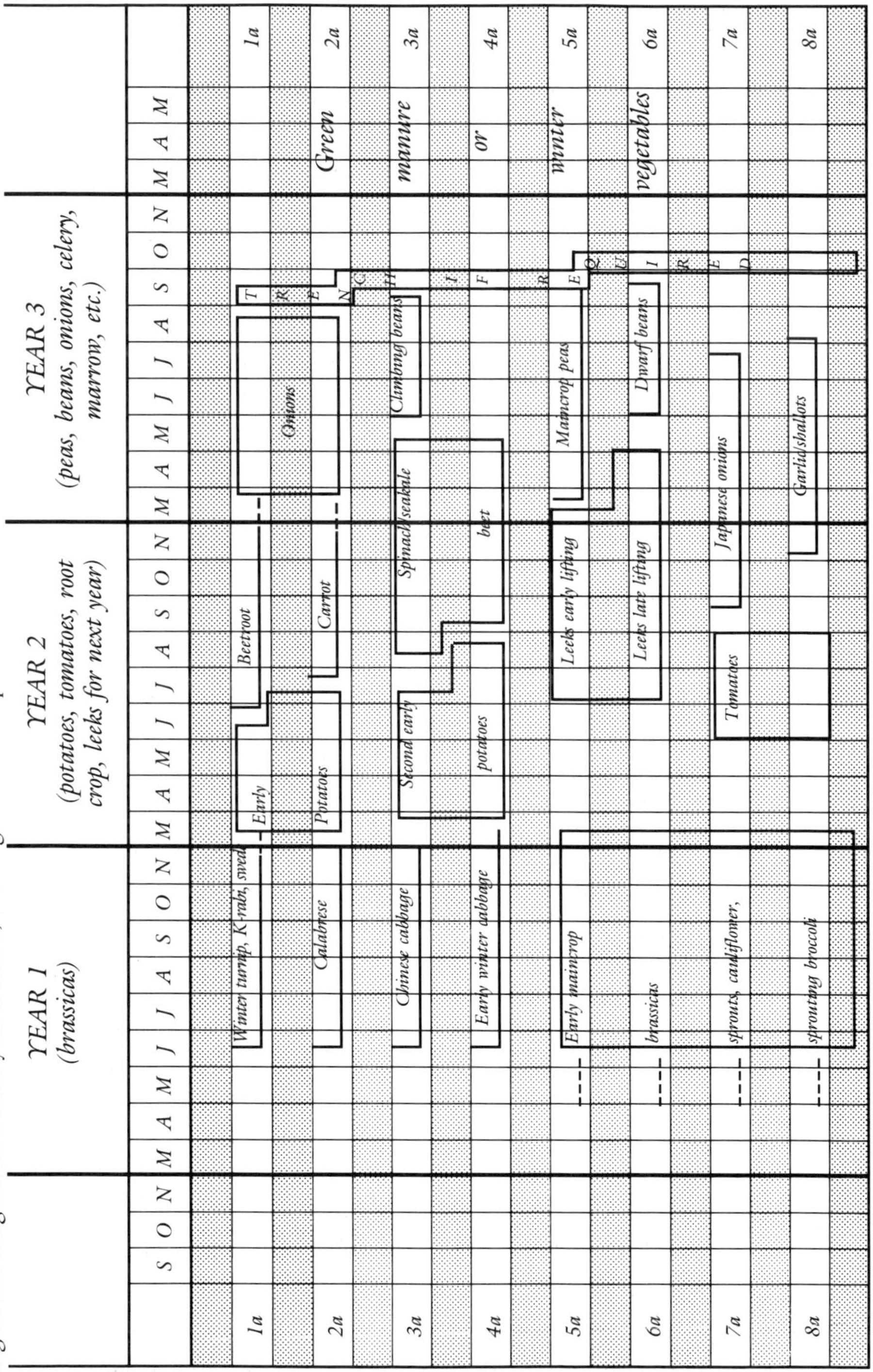
YEAR 1
(brassicas)
YEAR 2
(potatoes, tomatoes, root crop, leeks for next year)
YEAR 3
(peas, beans, onions, celery, marrow, etc.)
S O N M A M J J A S O N M A M J J A S O N M A M J J A S O N M A M
1a
2a
3a
4a
5a
6a
7a
8a
Winter turnip, K-rabi, swede
Calabrese
Chinese cabbage
Early winter cabbage
Early maincrop
brassicas
sprouts, cauliflower,
sprouting broccoli
Early
Potatoes
Beetroot
Carrot
Second early
potatoes
Spinach/seakale
beet
Leeks early lifting
Leeks late lifting
Tomatoes
Japanese onions
Garlic/shallots
Onions
Climbing beans
Maincrop peas
Dwarf beans
TRENCH
FIRE
QUIRED
Green
manure
or
winter
vegetables

Figure 42: Diagram of a three-year rotation, showing the main crops

1b 2b 3b 4b 5b 6b 7b 8b

S O N M A M J J A S O N M A M J J A S O N M A M J J A S O N M A M

Winter turnips, kohlrabi, swede — Broad beans late picked — Finocchio

Late winter cabbage — Beans early picked — Celery

Kale — Maincrop potatoes — Hardy early picked — Celeriac

Late maincrop — Peas late picked — Marrow

brassicas — Scorzonera — Courgette

sprouts — Salsify — Cucumber

cauliflower — Parsnip — Sweetcorn

sprouting broccoli — Jerusalem artichoke — Summer celery

Green manure or winter vegetables

Winter vegetables

1b 2b 3b 4b 5b 6b 7b 8b

Note: summer vegetables can be planted in the gaps between the main rows, as well as in the intercropping rows

Figure 43: Three-year rotation giving a six-year rotation for potatoes

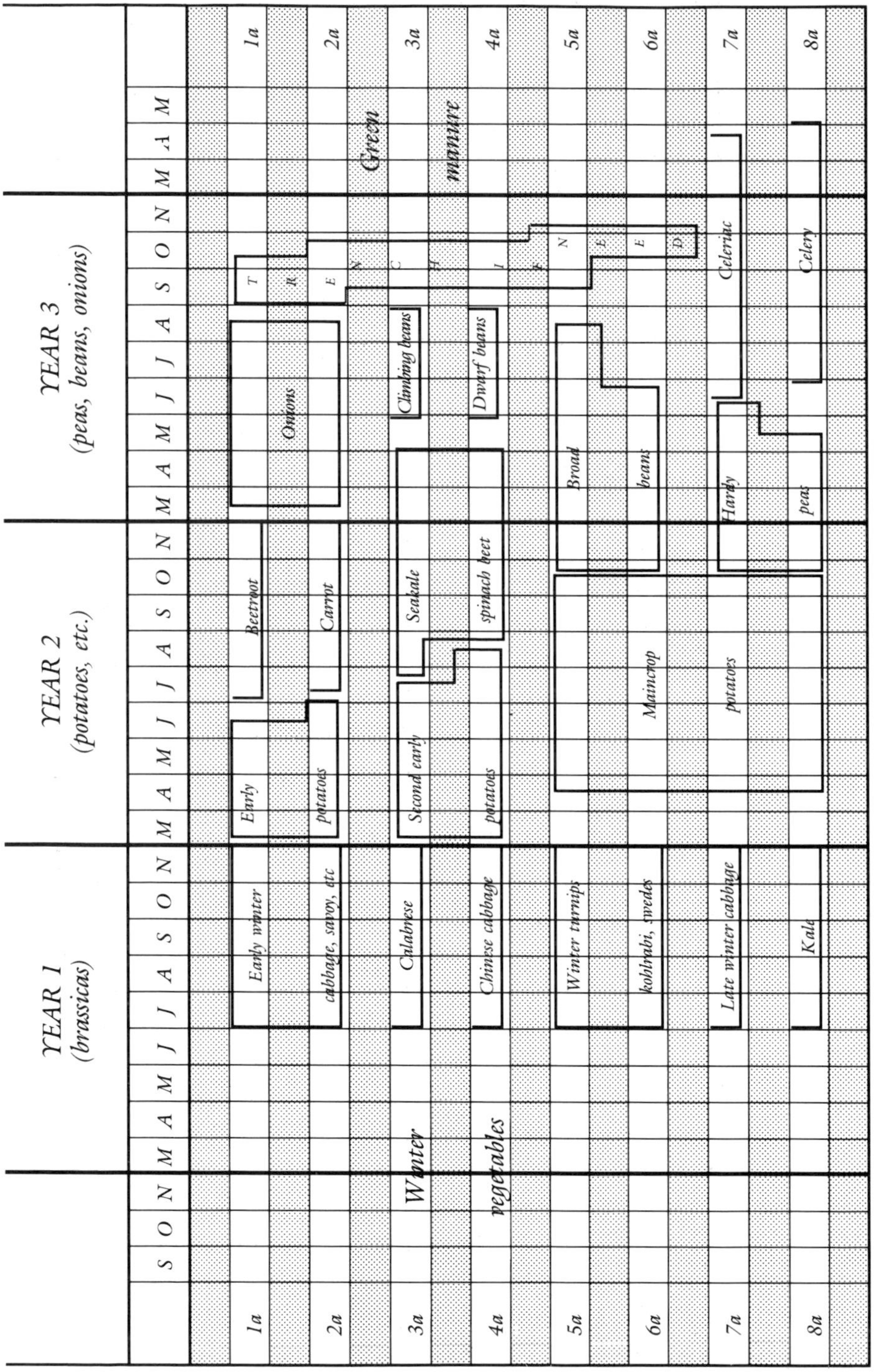

	S	O	N	M	A	M	J	J	A	S	O	N	M	A	M	J	J	A	S	O	N	M	A	M	J	J	A	S	O	N	M	A	M	
1b											Scorzonera																					Winter		1b
2b												Salsify							Marrow															2b
3b													Parsnip						etc.													vegetables		3b
4b													Jerusalem artichoke																					4b
5b					Early winter	brassicas											Leeks			Mizuna/crop peas														5b
6b																			Japanese onions															6b
7b						Late winter	brassicas			Tomatoes										Finocchio														7b
8b													Shallots/garlic																					8b

Green manure

take precedence over an edible crop, if one can be grown, providing your soil is not in such a sorry state that its rehabilitation is the major priority.

Having worked out your main crops, then start to plan your smaller summer and winter crops. Most of the factors discussed in previous chapters and applied to the four-year rotation (distances apart, growing within the fertile band, interspersing them between the main crops and so on) apply equally to the three-year rotation, so it is not difficult to decide where these smaller crops would best fit in.

If you have large areas in your garden devoted to asparagus and strawberries it would probably be better to bring these into your rotation – certainly so in the case of strawberries. Figure 44 shows the rotation for this:

Year 1: strawberries are planted out in August after early potatoes (as in the four-year rotation)

Year 2: first year crop

Year 3: second-year crop – they can then be lifted in July to be followed by, say, winter cabbage, or lifted in August, to be followed by spring cabbage or Chinese cabbage, or they can be left in for another year.

Year 4: crop and lift in July to be followed by leeks or lift in August/September to be followed by some autumn-sown crop (hardy peas or Japanese onions, etc.).

Asparagus can also be grown in a three-year rotation, sowing in the spring of the potato year and retained until the fourth year and lifted in July or August. Strawberries and asparagus can both be incorporated as in a four-year rotation, and you will get the familiar repeat of rows as shown in Figure 45.

You will see that in a three-year rotation the inclusion of asparagus does not give you an extra row because the ninth row is used up throughout the rotation by the asparagus; the inclusion of strawberries can give you an extra row though, if you lift them in July of the third year and follow them with one of the July-planted winter brassicas. Strawberries will also give you an extra potato row because they can follow the early potato crop but asparagus cannot because they have to be sown in the spring. However, as the plots already have eight rows, the need for those extra rows for brassicas and potatoes may not be so pressing.

So, what conclusion can we come to – is the four-year rotation or the

Year		1	2	3	4	5	6	7	
	Row 1	1	2	3	(4)				
P	Row 2	P			P			P	1
L	Row 3	O			O			O	
O	Row 4	T			T			T	
T	Row 5	A			A			A	
	Row 6	T			T	1	2	3	T(4)
2	Row 7	O			O			O	
	Row 8	E			E			E	
	Row 9	S			S			S	

This diagram shows the rotation for strawberries in plot 2 over the first seven years. Each new planting is made in a different row, as widely spaced from the last one as possible, so that in year 1 you plant in row 1, in year 4 in row 6, in year 7 in row 2, in year 10 in row 7, and so on. This means that row 1 will not carry strawberries again until year 28. There will be similar successions in plots 1 and 3, always planting them in August in the potato year.

Figure 45: Three-year rotation for strawberries and asparagus together

	Year	1	2	3	4	5	6	7
	Row 1	1	2	3	(4)			
P	Row 2	P 1	2	3	P 4			P 1
L	Row 3	O			O			O 1
O	Row 4	T			T			T
T	Row 5	A			A			A
	Row 6	T			T 1	2	3	T(4)
2	Row 7	O			O 1	2	3	O 4
	Row 8	E			E			E
	Row 9	S			S			S
	Row 10							

Key:
123(4) strawberries
123 4 asparagus

three-year rotation the best option? The answer is, it depends quite a bit on your potato and brassica needs: think how many rows of them you want to grow; decide whether you are prepared to bring strawberries and asparagus into your rotation. You should then be able to judge whether you can fit everything you want to grow in to the quarter plots of your garden that a four-year rotation allows you. If you cannot you are faced with a choice: either you modify your needs, or you abandon the idea of a four-year rotation and opt for a three-year one, and there is always the option of not adhering to a strict rotation at all. Further than that I cannot help you – the decision is yours.

CHAPTER 14
KEEPING RECORDS

The serious gardener keeps records for two main purposes:

1. To be able to keep a check on how each part of the garden has been treated, what it has grown, when it has been limed or manured, for example, over the previous years.
2. So that the gardener can learn from experience, by a process of trial and error.

If you practise the system of fixed rows I am advocating in this book, the first of these is comparatively simple. You merely keep a list of each row and record what has happened to it each season. If you do not practise this system, it is probably easier to draw a plan of your garden for each season. I do not feel that there is any great benefit to be gained from detailed records of what is grown in each row, though broad areas of brassicas, potatoes, onions, and so on should be recorded. It is also, of course, important to keep a record of applications of compost or manure, applications of lime (which should be backed up by testing each year with a kit for measuring the acidity of the soil) and records of any rows that have been trenched. Also it is wise to keep a note of any special problems that have arisen or remedial action that needed to be taken. It is worth retaining these records for several years – you never know when you may want to refer back to them.

With regard to learning from experience it is worth bearing in mind the following: it is very difficult for one person growing a limited number of crops to assemble enough of the kind of information that is needed to provide sure guidelines; it is also difficult for an amateur, who does not have a background of expertise, to assess and interpret the results; it is also difficult to be sure that you have taken all the relevant facts and factors into account. As a result of this, although one may strike lucky and make useful discoveries, one can be easily misled.

Let us take an example. Suppose that you have a warm south-facing slope that, from previous observation, you decide is relatively frost-free and is, therefore, a good place to plant some very early potatoes. To test this you plant a short row in the first year as an experiment. It is a mild spring and the potatoes do very well. So in the following year, on the strength of this, you plant two long rows in the first week of March. Again, it is a mild spring and you see that your potatoes are growing well. When it comes to harvesting, however, your crop is disappointing – in fact, it turns out to be poor. There are no obvious signs of disease and you then realize that as well as a mild spring it has also been a relatively dry one and that the slope is rather sandy and dries out very quickly. Your potatoes were probably just lacking water – though you cannot be sure that this was the reason for their poor performance.

The following year you incorporate a good amount of compost into the soil in order to help it to retain moisture and, once again, you plant two rows. Early spring is wet, but even so you water whenever there are more than three or four days without rain. In mid May, with your potatoes showing a lot of healthy growth, there is a sharp cold spell. Your southern slope turns out to be not nearly so frost-free as you had thought and both rows are cut to the ground.

This is a very simple example of using your records. Some understanding of frosts and of the tendency of sandy soil to dry out was useful, but otherwise no great background of expertise was involved. The conclusion, however, that one year's trial was sufficient to justify two whole rows being risked the following year was perhaps premature. There are so many reasons why a crop may do well or badly, so many factors involved that it is extremely difficult to identify the key ones and, equally, to be certain how much (if at all) your own efforts have contributed to a particular result. One effect of this is that all kinds of 'rule-of-thumb' practices and remedies are regularly given without anyone really being sure that they are useful but, at the same time, neither are they sure that they should be dismissed as useless! The only way to improve our knowledge of these remedies is to test them scientifically. Many gardeners, especially organic gardeners, are sceptical of science and scientists, sometimes openly hostile. In particular, they associate science with the widespread over-use of pesticides and chemical fertilizers. I think we are right to be sceptical of individual scientists who use reductionist simplifications to validate their pet theories; but this does not invalidate a common-sense use of the scientific method to evaluate the success or otherwise of what we are doing.

This method involves three main factors: firstly, the elimination of incidental factors in any test procedure that may have influenced the results; secondly, consistent results over many trials indicating a clear benefit of one method over another under varying conditions; and, thirdly, a reasonable explanation of the processes involved. This is simply common sense but nonetheless a useful touch-stone for evaluating any claims made and also to check on any trials you yourself carry out.

There is one more thing to remember: although it is necessary to eliminate the incidentals in any tests or in assessing the results of tests, it is equally important to include them if you are recommending some procedure you have tested, because, of course, gardening does not take place in test conditions. For example, it is obvious that the techniques of pre-germinating seeds first published in the book *Know and Grow Vegetables*, worked very well in the conditions under which they were originally tested at the National Vegetable Research Station. It is equally obvious that the development and testing of this technique is of great benefit to gardeners and growers. But as I have noted previously, in transferring it to ordinary garden conditions one has to take into account the limitations of time, equipment and other resources with which most home gardeners work.

So, as a general rule, it is a good idea to keep records, to use them to judge how many rows of each crop you need to grow, which crops seem to suit your garden best, what grows well in various parts of your garden, which varieties you prefer, which are easiest to grow, which pests are particularly prevalent in your area and what success you have had in dealing with them, and so on. But, it is important to remember that the scale you are operating on is too small to provide conclusive results and to be cautious, not jumping to conclusions and keeping an open mind.

It is worth keeping records of:

Sowing and planting times and subsequent dates of harvesting crops and their quality;

Weather and any other factor that may have affected cropping;

Any problems that have occurred, how you dealt with them and how successfully you overcame them;

Number of plants or rows grown and how well they met your needs;

Time taken for seed pre-germination under various circumstances (e.g., in an airing cupboard).

There are two ways of keeping records that I have found easy to use. One is to keep a diary, entering the information by the date on which it occurs. The second way is to write notes under 'Crops' and other relevant headings. I do not think that one method has any inherent advantage over the other, it is a matter of personal preference, but probably a combination of the two is the most practical.

FURTHER READING

This book has been concerned with planning (although we have covered other subjects as they became relevant) and should be used alongside a general vegetable gardening book. There are hundreds of these and it is difficult to pick and choose between them, but here are some that I think you will find useful:

Dr D. G. Hessayon, *Vegetable Plotter* (Pan-Brittanica Industries). This is unashamedly pro-chemical but you can ignore that part of it if you do not like it. It is a very clear, simple and straightforward guide for the beginner.

Allan Jackson, *Observer Book of Vegetables* (Frederick Warne). A good, concise, fairly comprehensive book that you can comfortably slip in your pocket.

Sue Stickland, *Planning The Organic Herb Garden* (Thorsons). A book that challenges Claire Lowenfeld's classic *Herb Gardening* as the best book on this subject.

Lawrence Hills, *Organic Gardening* (Penguin). A smaller and cheaper book on the same lines as his vintage *Grow your Own Fruit and Vegetables*.

Lawrence Hills, *Save Your Own Seeds* (Henry Doubleday Research Association). This is a cheap booklet that is very well worth having if you aim to save seeds.

Dr Bleazard and Dr Salter (Eds.), *Know and Grow Vegetables* (Oxford University Press). The editors are from the National Vegetable Research Station, and the book was written by six research scientists. This book, unlike many gardening books, provides completely new information, supported by sound research. It is not a comprehensive gardening book that sets out to cover every gardening operation, but it throws important new light on the ones it does cover. It was followed by the equally original *Know and Grow Vegetables II*. I recommend them both to all serious gardeners.

The National Vegetable Research Station's *Gardener's Guides*. I recommend these – a list of those available can be obtained from:

The Librarian,
National Vegetable Research Station,
Wellesbourne,
Warwick CV35 9EF
(Enclose a stamped addressed envelope.)

Joy Larkcom, *Salad Garden* (Windward). Another book containing original material, it extends our knowledge of salad vegetables substantially. In this book I have only been able to cover the fringes of this subject, but Joy Larkcom's volume is a mine of mouthwatering information.

Jane Grigson, *Vegetable Cookbook* (Penguin). A good cookery book that does justice to the wide range of fresh, high quality, pesticide-free vegetables that I hope you will succeed in growing.

Lastly, my own book, *Composting* (Thorsons), complements Chapters 6 and 7 of this book.

SUPPLIERS

Alas, the range of vegetable seeds available from shops and from general mail order seed merchants diminishes yearly, and you may have difficulty tracking down some of the seeds mentioned in Chapter 3. However, there are still a number (a growing number, I believe) of specialist mail-order seed suppliers. Two of the best of these are:

Suffolk Herbs Sawyers Farm, Little Cornard, Sudbury, Suffolk CO10 OPF.
Heritage Seeds, Henry Doubleday Research Association, Ryton-on-Dunsmore, Coventry CV8 8LG.
Chase's Compost Seeds, Terminal House, Shepperton TW17 8AS.

Joy Larkcom's book, *Salad Garden*, contains useful lists of seed suppliers, organisations, and so on.

INDEX